GOING LIVE IN 3...2...1!

Tina Houser

©2009 by Warner Press Inc Anderson, IN 46012

www.warnerpress.org

Published by Warner Press Inc, Anderson, IN 46012

Warner Press and "WP" logo is a trademark of Warner Press, Inc

ISBN: 978-1-59317-356-2

Written by Tina Houser
Illustrations: Christian Elden
Editor: Karen Rhodes
Design and Layout: Kevin Spear
Printed in the USA

Warner Press Kids™
educate • nurture • inspire
www.warnerpress.org

CONTENTS

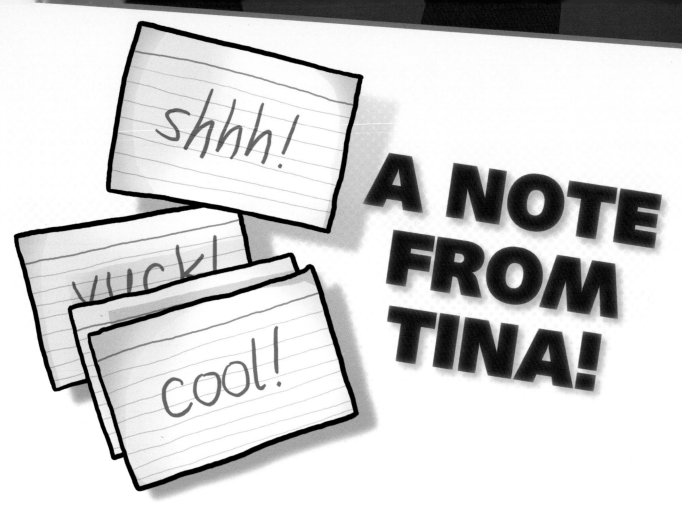

A NOTE FROM TINA!

My maternal grandmother was a storyteller at heart. As she got older the stories got wilder and funnier and bigger than life. When she started telling a whopper, we'd lower our heads and smirk at the addition of another extravagant detail that wasn't there the last time we heard that story. But no matter what you were thinking, you just couldn't resist closing out whatever else was going on so you could listen to what she had to say. Her love of everyday life and the people who made up that tapestry were her inspiration. Even though she's been gone for years now, when our family gathers, if someone gets carried away in the telling of a story or it leans a little on the unbelievable side, you're sure to hear somebody sarcastically say, "Okay, Grandma Bir!" She didn't leave much to her family as far as material possessions go, but I'm grateful that she left me with a love for telling the story.

There's a little plaything I sometimes purchase for object lessons or to give away as a prize in children's ministry; found in the toy department, they're usually called magic growing capsules. The fascination associated with these toys comes when one of the capsules is dropped into some warm water. Right before your eyes the capsule melts away and the little bit of spongy material inside takes on the water. Expanding and changing, the contents turn into a creature of some sort that comes to life in just moments. That's how I look at storytelling—a story captured in a capsule, waiting for the storyteller to add the warm water of a vivid imagination so that it comes to life for the listeners.

The Bible is full of intriguing stories that reveal the heart of God, but most of the time they're written in very few words or details. An entire story is often entrusted to just a few verses which serve as the capsule. In Matthew 9:19-22 we are told about a woman who had enormous faith in Jesus and exhibited that by reaching out to touch the hem of His garment for her healing. That beautiful event and Jesus' incredible reaction—all said in four little verses. What do those words tell us, though, about what that woman was feeling at the time? What do they tell us about the hardship, the ridicule, the ostracizing that went along with her condition? The storyteller's job is to mine those words diligently so that every ounce of emotion and context are uncovered, and then to present it so the listener will engage with the story. When that happens, the storyteller disappears within the story. That's exactly what we want—kids getting so wrapped up in the story that the storyteller and the method are secondary.

In Deuteronomy 6:20, we are all given a glimpse into our future. This verse tells us that children WILL ask us the meaning of the Scriptures. And when they do, Deuteronomy 6:21 tells us what to do, "Then you must tell them." It goes on to explain what the Israelites were to tell the children. It's the story! It's the story of how they were in captivity to the Egyptians and how God led them out of their slavery. How will future generations know about our Almighty God? They'll know when we tell them. And what do we tell them? We tell them the story, our personal story of how we were captive to sin and how God led us out of our slavery. And, we tell them all the other stories we find in the Bible of God's faithfulness.

I love the story in Joshua 4 where God draws back the waters of the Jordan River for the Israelites to cross into the Promised Land. Joshua instructs a representative of each tribe to pick up a stone from the river bed as they cross. On the other side they pile the rocks as a memorial. But what I love most is what the Scriptures say about why that memorial was built. Read it in Joshua 4:21-24 (NLT).

> *Then Joshua said to the Israelites, "In the future, your children will ask, 'What do these stones mean?' Then you can tell them, 'This is where the Israelites crossed the Jordan on dry ground.' For the Lord your God dried up the river right before your eyes, and he kept it dry until you were all across, just as he did at the Red Sea when he dried it up until we had all crossed over. He did this so that all the nations of the earth might know the power of the Lord, and that you might fear the Lord your God forever."*

Joshua had them build a memorial so the children would ask questions about their heritage as God's people. And then he tells them, when your kids do ask about this memorial, be ready—be ready—to tell them THE story. An effective storytelling technique leads children to ask questions rather than answers all their questions. This pile of stones would raise questions and it became the technique the Israelites could use to tell future generations God's story. A pile of rocks would intrigue the children and become an object lesson they would identify with the story. And, that, my dear friend, is what this book is about. It's about giving you those tools—those techniques—that will encourage children to ask questions and help them connect with the life-changing stories of the Bible.

In these pages you are going to find more than twenty different techniques you can employ to grab the attention of your kids so they'll enter into the story. Some will fit your personality and resources perfectly. Others will feel a little uncomfortable for you, at least at first. Stretch yourself to try each one at least once. It's like trying a new food; you don't know if you like it until you taste it. You also won't know its impact until you use it with your kids. So, give it a try! Two things I do want to caution you about. First of all, you'll find that a few of the techniques will become your favorites and you'll be tempted to use them all the time. Resist! A huge benefit to having so many techniques is that it keeps things mixed up for kids. It keeps the storytelling time fresh. They never know what to expect and that's a good thing. Using the same technique over and over will become old and predictable, which translates into kids losing interest. Shake it up and keep kids a little off-balance. Secondly, I've connected certain stories to specific techniques only to demonstrate how the technique can be used. That doesn't mean you can't try others. Every story can be told effectively in one of these ways, and I have by no means listed every Bible story.

Let your imagination loose as you read and then accept the challenge to become a better storyteller so the children you touch will comprehend the truth about God and the world they live in.

WHAT IS A STORY?

Did you know that stories have bones? Just like each of us has the same kind of bones in our body, stories have the same basic structure. What covers our bones makes us look different, and what is added to the basic structure of a story is what fleshes it out. Each story is different because of what covers the bones. One of the first steps to take in developing your storytelling skills is to understand what these bones are.

THERE IS A MAIN CHARACTER.

- This character has traits and characteristics with which the audience can identify.
- There's something about this character that draws the attention of the audience and they want to know more about him or her.

THE MAIN CHARACTER FACES AN OBSTACLE, A STRUGGLE.

- This obstacle may be difficulty in a relationship or some kind of physical problem he is dealing with.
- As the problem is described, the audience shares the emotion that the main character encounters because of the struggle.

THE MAIN CHARACTER MAKES A CHOICE.

- There is a change, decision or discovery made because of the obstacle he experienced.
- The character takes action to change the situation and the audience identifies with the action, whether favorably or not.

THE LIFE OF THE MAIN CHARACTER IS CHANGED.

- The choice the character makes changes his or her life in some way, and very well may change the lives of others also.
- The audience can identify the cause and effect—the character made this particular choice because of this particular obstacle and caused this particular change.

Understanding the parts that make up a story is important to the storyteller. Reviewing the *bones,* the basics with children after the story has been told is an excellent drill to make them aware of the vein of similarities that run through the biblical accounts. The repetition of identifying the *bones* is a great exercise and powerful lesson. Identify the main character, the obstacle (struggle), the choice and the change that occurred in the character and others affected by him or her. Hopefully, from each story the children will be able to draw a parallel of the Bible story to their own lives and recognize how they can learn from what happened to the characters in the story.

10 REASONS TO BECOME A GOOD STORYTELLER

1. DECREASES DISCIPLINE PROBLEMS

When kids are focused on the storyteller, they aren't distracted by other people in the room or looking for something fun to do. They aren't bored but are engaged by the story and the person sharing it.

2. INCREASES RETENTION

Because they've been drawn into the story—not distracted, they're listening closely and their minds are focusing on the story. Naturally, they are going to retain more of the story because that's what they're thinking about.

3. MAKES IT MORE FUN TO TEACH

When kids are enjoying themselves and you know they are learning, teaching is a lot more rewarding and a lot more fun. It's like the difference between kids eating something they like and being force-fed creamed beets. There is so much satisfaction in knowing they're enjoying learning while you're enjoying teaching.

4. ENABLES US TO SEE THINGS FROM A DIFFERENT PERSPECTIVE

Upon hearing a story, the listener identifies his obstacle (challenge) as similar to that of the main character. The choice the character made may not be the same perspective the listeners had on their particular situation, but hopefully, it will be enlightening. The similarity between decisions, though, can also serve as affirmation that listeners are doing what God would want them to do.

5. ENCOURAGES US TO SUBMIT

Storytelling helps the audience take to heart the consequences of turning away from God and the benefits of submitting to Him. Recognizing these benefits within the story encourages children to give God control of their lives.

6. REVEALS THE WILL OF GOD

By recognizing how they fit into the story, children can start to see what God's will is for their lives.

7. PROVIDES A BASE FOR LATER DECISIONS

Quite often my husband, who is a senior pastor, spends much of his sermon time reviewing what I would consider a well-known story from the Bible. He does so because many in the congregation do not have basic knowledge of the Bible stories. If good storytelling enables retention, then kids will be able to "connect the dots" by referring to what they know of the Bible when they have important decisions to make.

8. CONNECTS US TO HISTORY

We each have several history trees. We have our family tree that tells us the people we have descended from and the struggles they went through to make our lives possible. We have a national history that identifies us as a people by what we have accomplished together, both those of the present and those from the past. Then, we have our spiritual history which connects us to all those faithful people who have gone before us.

9. REVEALS THE KINGDOM OF GOD

Jesus made up stories that we call parables. Each one unveiled something about the kingdom of God. Good storytelling helps kids understand a little better what God meant by His kingdom.

10. SPREADS THE GOSPEL OF JESUS CHRIST

Good storytelling challenges listeners to make a decision for Christ because of what Jesus did for us all. The listener becomes the main character who has a dilemma and makes choices that change his or her life.

DIRECTOR'S NOTES:

When you ask, "Would anybody like to help act out our story today?" There are going to be hands going up everywhere if your kids are anything like the kids I work with. There will be a few timid ones, but one of the strengths of this technique is that it's not only fun to be one of the actors, it's also fun to watch what your friends are doing.

Using actors is always more successful if there are a few simple costumes and some appropriate props, so read through the story once specifically with that in mind, and then consider what you already have at your disposal.

An alternative way of doing this, especially with a large group, is to recruit some junior and senior high youth to be your actors. They usually have fond memories of being in children's ministry and would like to come back for a visit. And, these youth have a tremendous influence on the younger kids when they serve as role models and mentors.

SCRIPT 1 - God Cares for Elijah (1 Kings 16:29—17:16)

PROPS:

- Costume for Elijah – robe
- Costume for King Ahab – crown and a royal cape

- Costume for woman – a robe and shawl

- Costume for raven – black boa to drape across the shoulders and down arms, a rubber bird beak

- Piece of bread

- Stream - light blue plastic tablecloth

- Sticks for the woman to pick up

- Jars for flour and oil

CAST:

King Ahab, Elijah, soldiers of the king, a woman, a raven

SCENE 1:

- King Ahab was a terrible king. He worshiped idols and let his wife, Jezebel talk him into building temples to her strange gods. (*King Ahab stands up front.*)

- One day, God sent Elijah to stand before King Ahab with a message. (*Elijah moves to confront Ahab.*)

- Elijah told Ahab there would be no more dew or rain until God decided to send more. (*Elijah shakes his finger at Ahab.*)

- Ahab seemed unaffected by Elijah's news and Elijah left the king's presence. (*Elijah quickly walks away.*)

- Sure enough, there was no dew and there was no rain. That's when Ahab remembered what Elijah said. (*King Ahab puts his finger to his head as if remembering, an "aha" moment.*)

- So, Ahab sent his soldiers all over the kingdom looking for Elijah, but they couldn't find him anywhere. (*The soldiers walk around the room, looking under and behind pieces of furniture.*)

SCENE 2:

- Knowing that Ahab would try to find Elijah, God told Elijah to go to the stream and wait there. (*Elijah goes to the plastic blue tablecloth.*)

- The stream provided water for Elijah. (*Elijah drinks from the stream.*)

- And God sent ravens to Elijah each morning and each evening with bread and meat. (*The raven will "fly" by and drop the piece of bread from its beak near Elijah.*)

SCENE 3:

- Because there had been no rain, one day the stream dried up. (*Pull the blue plastic away.*)

- Elijah didn't know what he should do now. He prayed and God told him to go into the nearby town. As he entered the town, he found the woman God said would be there picking up sticks. (*Position woman off to the side picking up sticks on the floor.*)

- God had taken care of things.

SCENE 4:

- When Elijah came to town, he noticed a poor woman gathering sticks. (*Elijah walks over to the woman.*)

- This must be the woman God was talking about. When Elijah asked her for some water and food, she was perplexed. (*Woman gives Elijah a questioning look.*)

- She explained that she had only a little bit of flour and oil. She was gathering sticks to make a fire so she could prepare a last meal for her and her son. (*Woman holds out her empty hands.*)

SCENE 5:

- Elijah told the woman that God would provide her flour and oil throughout the famine, if she prepared a cake for him along with the cakes she was making for her and her son. (*Woman pours from jars and pretends to make cakes.*)

- She made the cakes just as Elijah said and the jars never became empty. (*She looks into jars and is astonished.*)

- There was always enough for another meal.

For more scripts, visit www.warnerpress.org/321.html

DIRECTOR'S NOTES:

Another aspect of acting out a story involves groups of people participating in the story, such as the disciples, the Israelites or a crowd. The entire audience becomes part of the story by acting out their group part, with each person portraying his or her individual personality. In a crowd following Jesus through the streets, there were probably people who listened closely while others shouted to get Jesus' attention. There were those who cautiously stayed close to Jesus, taking small steps each time He moved, keeping their front row seat intact. In contrast, there were those who pushed and shoved their way through the crowd, doing whatever they felt necessary to get close. You may want to give cue cards to some of the children to guide them in what they might say or do as part of the story.

Here is an example of everyone participating as actors in the story.

SCRIPT 2 - Last Supper (Matthew 26:17-30; Mark 14:12-26; Luke 22:3-39; John 13)

CAST:

- Jesus
- Peter
- Judas - This can be an adult or older child who has been clued beforehand.
- Other disciples - the rest of the children—no matter if there are six or sixteen.

SETTING:

It would be wonderful if the location for the story could actually be in a room upstairs.

PROPS:

- Set the room up beforehand by folding the legs of a long table under and then resting the table on some concrete blocks. This lifts the table off the ground about nine inches.
- Cover the table with a loosely woven cloth.
- A grapevine wreath, candles, goblets or clay cups and clay jars can be placed on the table.

- Grapes, bread, juice, nuts, apples and other food of that day can be placed on the table also.

- A basin of water and some towels should be easily accessible.

- The candles should be lit and the lights turned low when the children walk up the stairs.

DIRECTOR'S NOTES:

As you're heading to the stairs tell the children how Jesus had sent Peter and John into the city to find a man carrying a pitcher of water. They were to ask the man about a guest room where Peter and John were to make preparations for the Passover meal for Jesus and the disciples.

Once everyone has entered the room, the storyteller will describe the events that took place in there in the following manner:

SCENE 1:

(The children will recline around the table with the three actors among them.)

- Early in the story Jesus gets up and goes to the basin of water, takes off His outer garment and ties a towel around His waist.

- He proceeds to wash the feet of the disciples. The actor playing Jesus will do this to as many of the children as want to participate.

- The storyteller talks about how Jesus and Peter engage in conversation when Peter wants his hands and head to be washed also.

- When Jesus recognizes His betrayer, the actor playing Jesus will dip the bread and hand it to the actor playing Judas.

- Upon receiving the bread, Judas abruptly leaves the room.

SCENE 2:

- The storyteller describes how Jesus and the disciples shared a meal together, so encourage the children to eat the food that is on the table.

- As they start to eat, talk about how Jesus described the significance of the bread and the juice.

- Once Jesus had given thanks He handed each disciple a piece of the bread, so the actor should do likewise.

- Although the Scriptures say the cup was passed, give the children individual cups of juice that they can drink at the dinner.

SCENE 3:

- After dinner was over, this part of the evening came to a close as the disciples left the upper room, singing a song together.

(Choose a song the children know well and sing it together as they exit.)

DIRECTOR'S NOTES:

Can you see what a powerful experience this can be for children? It takes a little planning. It takes a little effort on the part of the actors. And, it takes some extra preparation to get all the elements and table set. But, what an impact it will make!

For more scripts, visit www.warnerpress.org/321.html

DIRECTOR'S NOTES:

This technique is used when there is a recurring action in the story. Look for stories where there is some form of repetition happening at least three times. Recognize repetition within the story then create a rhyme that restates what's happening or being said. These rhymes need to be very simple in nature and have a strong downbeat. Then, before telling the story, teach the rhyme to the audience and review it several times so they know it from memory. Each time the storyteller comes to a place in the story where the repetitive action or response occurs, he or she will signal the audience to insert the rhyme. Their rhyme responses should flow in and out of the story without fanfare or pause.

SCRIPT 1 - Paul Travels with a Message (Acts 13:13—16:5)

DIRECTOR'S NOTES:

It's not terribly important for children to be able to name every town and city that Paul traveled to, but what is important is that at each one of those places Paul did the same thing. He preached the message of Jesus to them: how Jesus lived among them, teaching them about God, how He died and was resurrected, and how through Jesus we can be forgiven of our sins.

Turn it up!

Turn up your enthusiasm. Turn up your passion. Turn up your conviction to communicate the truth of God's Word. If you're excited about telling the story, you've increased the possibility that the kids will be excited about listening to it.

Teach the children this rhyme.

> **Paul had a message.**
> **The message was the same.**
> **Every time he had the chance**
> **Paul preached in Jesus' name.**

Paul went to Antioch where he was asked to speak on the Sabbath in the synagogue. And…

> **Paul had a message.**
> **The message was the same.**
> **Every time he had the chance**
> **Paul preached in Jesus' name.**

The Jewish leaders in the synagogue did not like what Paul was saying, but the Gentiles wanted to hear more, so Paul spoke to them the next Sabbath. And…

> **Paul had a message.**
> **The message was the same.**
> **Every time he had the chance**
> **Paul preached in Jesus' name.**

Paul was eventually chased out of Antioch so he traveled on to Iconium. In Iconium, Paul spoke to Jews and Gentiles, and many of them believed, because…

> **Paul had a message.**
> **The message was the same.**
> **Every time he had the chance**
> **Paul preached in Jesus' name.**

But, some of the people didn't like what Paul was saying, so they ran him out of Iconium. That didn't stop Paul. He traveled on to Lystra, where…

> **Paul had a message.**
> **The message was the same.**
> **Every time he had the chance**
> **Paul preached in Jesus' name.**

Even though some people in Lystra beat Paul and left him to die, Paul got back up. He traveled on to Derbe and guess what? He preached to whoever would listen there, and…

> **Paul had a message.**
> **The message was the same.**
> **Every time he had the chance**
> **Paul preached in Jesus' name.**

SCRIPT 2 - Jesus Calls the Disciples (Mark 1:16-38; Mark 2:14-17)

DIRECTOR'S NOTES:

There's very little to the story of Jesus calling His disciples, but it's important for the children to get the idea of what happened. Each of these people dropped what they were doing to be with Jesus. The Bible tells us little more than that when Jesus called them, they left, they followed. He called others—they left, they followed. So, teach the children this rhyme to recite as the response to Jesus approaching each person. For added fun, include the taps indicated, which can be done by hitting two sticks together or simply clapping your hands.

> *He (They) left his (their) business and walked away*
> *to follow Jesus each and every day.*
> *Uh-huh (tap, tap), Uh-huh (tap, tap)*
> *Uh-huh (tap, tap), Uh-huh (tap, tap)*

Part of God's plan was for Jesus to teach a small group of people, who we refer to as the disciples, so that when Jesus returned to heaven, they would continue preaching and teaching His message. One day as Jesus walked along the shore of the Sea of Galilee, He began to bring that special group of men together. Jesus looked up and saw two brothers, Andrew and Simon, working at their fishing business. He yelled out to them, "Come, follow me, and I will make you fishers of men." So…

> *He (They) left his (their) business and walked away*
> *to follow Jesus each and every day.*
> *Uh-huh (tap, tap), Uh-huh (tap, tap)*
> *Uh-huh (tap, tap), Uh-huh (tap, tap)*

Jesus continued walking down the shore until He came to another boat where two more brothers, James and John, were mending their nets. Again Jesus called out, "Come, follow me, and I will make you fishers of men." So…

> *He (They) left his (their) business and walked away*
> *to follow Jesus each and every day.*
> *Uh-huh (tap, tap), Uh-huh (tap, tap)*
> *Uh-huh (tap, tap), Uh-huh (tap, tap)*

On another day, Jesus was walking through the city of Capernaum where He saw a man named Matthew collecting taxes. Matthew was not a popular man because tax collectors were known for taking more money from the people than the government required them to collect. When Jesus looked at Matthew, though, He did not see what other people saw. So Jesus said, "Matthew, follow me," and…

He (They) left his (their) business and walked away
to follow Jesus each and every day.
Uh-huh (tap, tap), Uh-huh (tap, tap)
Uh-huh (tap, tap), Uh-huh (tap, tap)

SCRIPT 3 - Moses Approaches Pharaoh (Exodus 7:14 — 10:29)

Moses went to Pharaoh to request that the Israelites be allowed to journey into the desert to worship. Each time Moses approached Pharaoh and asked him to let the people go, Pharaoh refused to consider it. Then God sent a sign (*turned blood to water, frogs, lice, fleas, flies, cattle disease, boils, hail, locusts, angel of death*)—ten of them. And each time Pharaoh begged Moses to pray that God would take it away, promising to let the people go to pray. Then, when each plague was lifted, Pharaoh's heart hardened and he once again refused.

DIRECTOR'S NOTES:

Divide the children into two groups.

The first group will learn the following rhyme:

> **Pharaoh, Pharaoh,**
> **let my people go.**

The second group will say:

> **You will never leave here!**
> **No, no, no!**

Each time you come to a place in the story where Moses approached Pharaoh, point to the first group. As soon as the first group finishes, say, "And Pharaoh responded…" Then the second group will say their rhyme. Encourage the second group to raise their fists in the air when they say, "No, no, no!" It's important to keep these two segments tight, with very little delay between them so that the rhyme comes through.

For more scripts that use rhyming, visit www.warnerpress.org/321.html

DIRECTOR'S NOTES:

In this technique, the children will question what you have just said in the telling of the story. They'll know what to ask because they are shown prompting cards. Then, when they have asked the question in unison, you will answer the question by saying "Yes" and complete it by repeating what they questioned. *(That sounds confusing as I write it, but it's really a fairly simple and effective technique, so stick with me through the example.)*

PROPS:

- Beforehand, go through the story and choose places that the children could question.

- Make up large cue cards or PowerPoint™ slides with the questions on them, keeping them in order.

- Keep a list of the questions to refer to as you tell the story.

SCRIPT 1 - Abram Goes Where God Sends Him
(Genesis 11:27 — 12:20)

Leader: Abram and his family lived in a place called Haran. Because Abram's brother had died, Abram took care of his nephew, Lot.

Children: His nephew was Lot?

Leader: Yes, his nephew was Lot.

Leader: One day, God spoke to Abram and told him to leave that place and take his family to a new land that God would show him.

Children: God told him to move?

Leader: Yes, God told him to move.

Leader: God also told Abram that He would make him a great blessing to all the families of the world. What God meant was that the Savior of the World, Jesus, would be born through one of Abram's descendants.

Children: The blessing was Jesus?

Leader: Yes, the blessing was Jesus.

Leader: So Abram took his wife Sarai, his nephew Lot, his servants and all the flocks and started on a journey. God would lead them to their new home.

Children: God would lead them to their new home?

Leader: Yes, God would lead them to their new home.

Leader: They traveled across the desert. They went across rivers. They walked through valleys and over hills. Each day they got closer to the land that God had planned for their new home.

Children: They journeyed to their new home?

Leader: Yes, they journeyed to their new home.

Leader: When they got to the plain of Moreh, God spoke to Abram again and told him this was the place. The land was called Canaan and it was their new home.

Children: Their new home was Canaan?

Leader: Yes, their new home was Canaan.

Leader: Abram built an altar there and worshiped God, thanking Him for bringing them to this wonderful place.

Children: Abram built an altar to God?

Leader: Yes, Abram built an altar to God.

Leader: Abram and his family and servants lived in tents outside the cities where they could get plenty of grass for the flocks. The flocks and herds got larger and larger and Abram became a rich man.

Children: Abram was rich?

Leader: Yes, Abram was rich.

Leader: After Abram had lived in Canaan for a while, there was a famine. No rain fell and the grass did not grow. Abram picked up his tents and his household and moved to Egypt where they could find water. When the famine was over they moved back to Canaan once again.

Children: Abram followed God?

Leader: Yes, Abram followed God…and God took care of him and his family.

SCRIPT 2 - Nehemiah Rebuilds the Wall (Nehemiah 2:19—6:19)

Leader: Nehemiah heard that Jerusalem was in shambles.

Children: Jerusalem was in shambles?

Leader: Yes, Jerusalem was in shambles.

Leader: The first thing he did was fast and pray.

Children: He fasted and prayed?

Leader: Yes, he fasted and prayed.

Leader: Then, King Artaxerxes noticed that Nehemiah was sad.

Children: Nehemiah was sad?

Leader: Yes, Nehemiah was sad.

Leader: King Artaxerxes didn't want Nehemiah to be sad so he sent him to Jerusalem with letters that would keep him safe.

Children: Letters that would keep him safe?

Leader: Yes, letters that would keep him safe.

Leader: Nehemiah gave everyone jobs to do.

Children: Everyone had jobs to do?

Leader: Yes, everyone had jobs to do.

Leader: But Sanballat and Tobiah made fun of Nehemiah and said that if a fox walked on the wall it would surely tumble down.

Children: They said it would surely tumble down?

Leader: Yes, they said it would surely tumble down.

Leader: Each worker held a spear in one hand and worked with the other, because Sanballat and Tobiah were planning to attack.

Children: Planning to attack?

Leader: Yes, planning to attack.

Leader: The workers finished the wall around Jerusalem in 52 days.

Children: In 52 days?

Leader: Yes, in 52 days.

Leader: When all the work was done, the people celebrated by worshiping God. They read scripture, ate and had a festival.

Children: Read scripture, ate and had a festival?

Leader: Yes, read scripture, ate and had a festival.

DIRECTOR'S NOTES:

Kids love black lights! So, why not use them in storytelling? This technique takes the traditional flannelgraph and kicks it up a couple of notches.

PROPS:

A few pieces of simple equipment are needed to pull off a black light story.

- First of all, you'll need a **black light**. (That was brilliant!) These can be purchased for under $25 in the electrical/lighting section at most discount department stores. They come in a variety of sizes, but the larger the black light, the better the effect. Then, you'll also need a lightweight board that has been covered in black flannel, felt or fleece. An old portable bulletin board works great as the base.

- For each story you'll need to make **cut-outs** of people and objects in the story. These figures can be found in old coloring books or used curriculum. The best resource I have found, though, is a set of two books called *Old Testament Bible Story Patterns* and *New Testament Bible Story Patterns* by Sherrill Flora, published by In Celebration. The stories are listed in the front of the book along with the figures needed. Once you've located the figures, copy them onto heavy fluorescent paper, preferably card stock. Enlarge them according to the size of your display board. Cut the figures out and then apply a piece of Velcro™ (the prickly side, not the loops) to the back of each figure. (Figures have been provided for the two scripts seen here. You will need to cut them out, enlarge them, if you wish, then copy on fluorescent paper.)

- You're now ready to gather the kids in a room that has been sealed from outside light. Wear dark clothing the day you use this technique; white clothes will glow in the dark and distract the students. Turn on the black light and let the figures glow in the dark as you tell another story of people who faithfully followed God. (If you have beautiful white teeth, don't be surprised when your smile lights up!)

SCRIPT 1 - Nicodemus Comes to Jesus at Night (John 3:1-21)

PROPS:

- A figure for Jesus

- A figure for Nicodemus

- Before the story starts the children can create the setting by placing figures on the board, such as:

  - Palm trees
  - Moon
  - Stars

  - A water jar
  - A couple of houses

DIRECTOR'S NOTES:

Nicodemus came to Jesus at night, so he must have wanted to keep his visit with Jesus a secret. When Nicodemus decides to go to Jesus, you can **move the figure around the end of one house as if he's looking around to see if anyone sees him.**

John 3:20-21 is very appropriate for a black light story because it talks about people who stay away from the light for fear their sins will be exposed. Even though the room is dark, the black light exposes even the tiniest pieces of lent.

SCENE 2 - Jesus Calms the Storm (Matthew 8:23-27; Mark 4:35-41; Luke 8:22-25)

PROPS:

- Boat
- Some lightning bolts
- Lightning bolt coming out of a cloud
- Groups of disciples that can be put on the boat
- Reclining Jesus
- Standing Jesus
- Rough waves
- A strip that represents the calm water.

DIRECTOR'S NOTES:

As you begin the story, **place the boat on the calm water.** The **standing Jesus** starts the story, because He is talking with the disciples.

- *Jesus was tired from being with the crowds of people all day, so He went to lie down.* **(Replace the standing Jesus with reclining Jesus.)**

- *A storm came up, but it didn't wake Him.* (**Add lightning and replace the calm water with the rough water.** When the disciples wake Jesus because they are afraid, **replace the reclining Jesus with the standing Jesus.** Then, when Jesus speaks to the storm, **replace the rough waves with the calm water.**)

OTHER STORIES TO USE WITH A BLACK LIGHT:

- The Angel Appears to the Shepherds (Luke 2:8-20)
- Jesus Walks on the Water (Matthew 14:23-36; Mark 6:47-56; John 6:16-29)
- An Earthquake Rocks the Tomb (Matthew 28:1-15; Mark 16:1-11; Luke 24:1-12; John 20:1-18)
- The Crucifixion (Matthew 27:1-54; Mark 15:1-39; Luke 23:1-47; John 18:28—19:30)
- Gideon Leads the Attack (Judges 7:1—8:28). Each child could have a flame to put on the board when the battle cry goes out to break the pitchers.

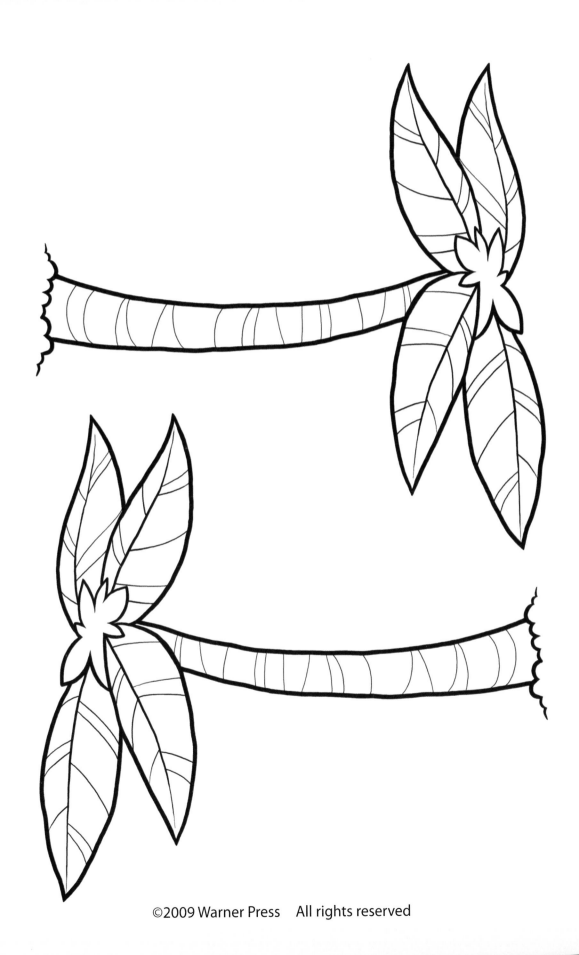

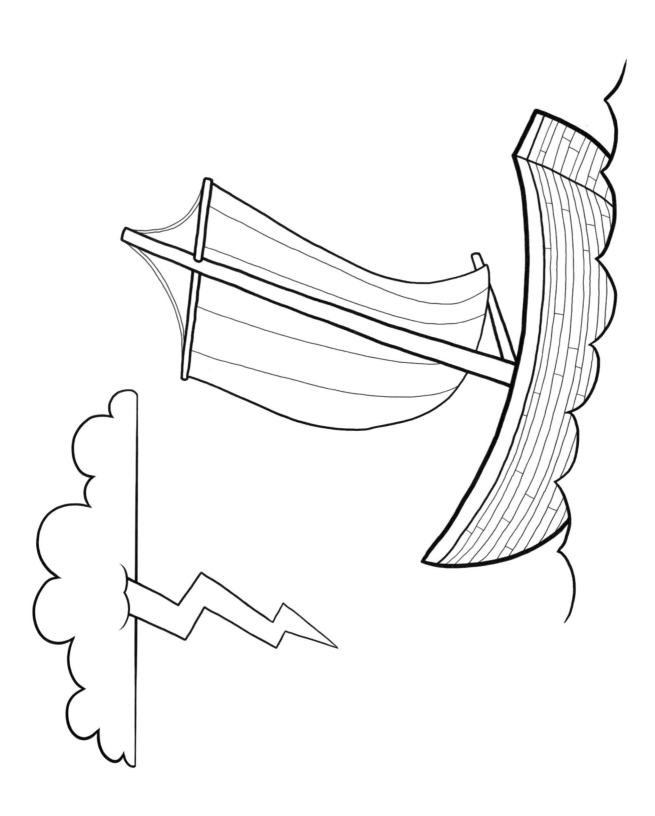

DIRECTOR'S NOTES:

Bonkers are 5-foot inflatable tubes, but they're actually more often called bongo sticks. These inflatable tubes can be purchased in dozens by searching for "inflatable bongo sticks" online. Most novelty companies carry them for approximately $6.50/dozen and they come in an assortment of colors. Another item that can be used in place of bongo sticks are pool noodles. They bend easily and can be purchased in a variety of colors for under $2.00.

In this technique, the children each receive a bonker. During the telling of the story, there will be scripted places where the storyteller will pause. At that point the children will portray something about the story using the bonker. You may have something in mind that you think they'll create, but get ready to be surprised by their creativity. Remember, there are no wrong answers, but you may need to ask a student to tell you about what they have created (in case you can't figure it out on your own). Some stories lend themselves to using the bonkers in small group settings and working together while other stories are best done as individuals. We'll show you one of each here.

In preparation for this, go through the story that you'll be telling and mark the pause points. These will be high action points or where an interesting object is mentioned.

USING BONKERS IN SMALL GROUPS

SCRIPT 1 - Joseph Is Sold into Slavery (Genesis 37)

SCENE 1:

Jacob had twelve sons, but one of them was more near and dear to his heart than the others. His name was Joseph, and Joseph could do no wrong in his father's eyes. As a demonstration of his special love for Joseph, Jacob had a colorful coat made for Joseph. **Pause** (Idea: a striped coat can be made from several bonkers draped around one of the children.)

Not only were the brothers jealous of the special treatment Joseph received from their father they were also angered by the dreams Joseph had. He had one dream where the wheat sheaves of the brothers bowed down to his sheaf. **Pause.** (Idea: fold the bonkers in half to make a sheaf and place them bowing down to one of the children.)

Then, there was another dream where the sun, moon and eleven stars bowed before Joseph. The dreams seemed to say that Joseph would become much greater than his brothers and they surely didn't like that.

SCENE 2:

One day the ten older brothers took the flocks of sheep and went away to find good pasture and water for them. After they had been gone for a while, Jacob sent Joseph to check on the brothers. When they saw the colorful coat coming their way, the brothers came up with a plan to get rid of Joseph. They decided to throw him in a cistern and leave him there to die. So, when Joseph arrived they grabbed him and threw him down in the pit. **Pause.** (Idea: together make a pit and put one person down in it.)

A caravan of merchants on camels came by on their way to a foreign land—Egypt. One of the sons had the idea to sell Joseph to the merchants in the camel caravan. **Pause.** (Idea: create camels with the bonkers.)

The merchants bought Joseph for twenty pieces of silver and took him away to be a slave in Egypt. **Pause.** (Idea: the children will probably depict something that resembles chains.)

USING BONKERS INDIVIDUALLY

SCRIPT 2 - Jesus Prays in the Garden of Gethsemane
(Matthew 26:36-46, Luke 22:39-53, John 18:1-11)

DIRECTOR'S NOTES:

After Jesus left the upper room where He shared the Passover meal with His disciples, He took the eleven to the Garden of Gethsemane. As they entered the garden, He told eight of the disciples to wait there and pray while He took Peter, James, and John with Him further into the garden. **Pause.** (Idea: the kids can come up with a variety of things here, such as, a tree in the garden, an entrance gate, folded praying hands, pointing at the disciples or motioning them to come.)

While Jesus prayed the disciples fell asleep. **Pause.** (Idea: roll the bonker to make a pillow.)

Twice Jesus woke them up and asked them to pray with Him. **Pause.** (Idea: make folded hands.)

While Jesus was praying alone God sent an angel to comfort Him. **Pause.** (Idea: create angel wings.)

Jesus knew what He was going to have to go through. He knew the cross was coming and He knew that all the sins of the world were about to be put on Him. Jesus prayed, "Father, if it's possible, let this pass away from me. But not what I want, your will should be done." **Pause.** (Idea: point to heaven.)

Jesus woke the disciples a third time. This time there was the sound of an angry crowd getting closer. The men were carrying torches in the dark of the night. **Pause.** (Idea: fold the bonkers and create a torch.)

Judas was in the crowd and stepped forward to kiss Jesus. That was the signal: Immediately the soldiers grabbed hold of Jesus to take Him away. Peter drew a sword and cut off the ear of one of the soldiers. **Pause.** (Idea: make a sword from the bonkers.)

Jesus healed the soldier's ear and then was taken away by the solders.

OTHER STORIES TO USE BONKERS WITH:

- The Faith of Four Friends (Matthew 9:2-8, Mark 2:1-12, Luke 5:18-26)

- Shadrach, Meshach, and Abednego (Daniel 3)

- Jeremiah Thrown in the Well (Jeremiah 37—52)

BONUS IDEA

Bonkers can also be used as rhythm instruments by folding them in half and then smacking the ends together. Or, they can be used for sound effects, such as when the crowd gets closer to the Garden of Gethsemane. The bonkers can make the sound of the heavy footsteps drawing near.

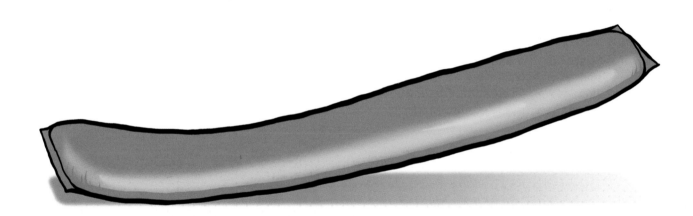

Mall O' Props

Props are great, but don't use props that may be distracting to the storytelling. Balloon sculpting is fun and can reinforce a point, but it's extremely difficult to keep the kids' attention on what you're saying when the actual demonstration is going on. If you want to add a fun prop, tell part of the story, add the prop and milk it for all it's worth, then let it disappear so you can finish the story.

CHANGE ENVIRONMENT

DIRECTOR'S NOTES:

Simply changing the surroundings gives storytelling freshness. Get out of your room…go outside…decorate an empty room in the church…take a field trip. We get in ruts and when we do, kids tune out. An uncomplicated change in the environment will hit the "on" button in kids' senses. Here are a couple of ideas for changing the environment and creating a memory.

SKIT 1 - Zacchaeus Wants to See Jesus (Luke 19:1-10)

DIRECTOR'S NOTES:

The church where I minister, until very recently, was located on Sycamore Street. The huge front lawn of the parsonage was shaded by four magnificent Sycamore trees—how convenient! When I contemplated how to tell the story of Zacchaeus, I couldn't pass up the opportunity to employ the Sycamore trees. I asked one of the men of the church to dress in biblical garb and sit in the tree, hidden by the gigantic Sycamore leaves. He was prepared to tell the story. The problem, though, was how to get the kids out on the front lawn.

Get to know the story

Think about each person—how she felt, what he saw, questions he may have had, his perspective, and how he reacted to what went on. Engage in an imaginary conversation with each person beforehand. Your discovery of the character will come out in the way you tell the story.

It was a beautiful spring Sunday morning, and about 5 minutes into our lesson I appeared fidgety to my students.

I started complaining about how pretty it was outside and how I really didn't want to be missing it by being stuck indoors. When I asked if they would like to pack up our stuff and move our lesson out to the parsonage front lawn, they didn't hesitate.

The children followed me across the parking lot and as we walked under the first Sycamore tree a booming voice yelled out of the tree.

"Hey! What are you kids doing?" Immediately, kids threw their heads back to look into the tree.

With jaws dropped and eyes wide, they exclaimed, "There's a man in our tree!"

I asked our Zacchaeus what he was doing in the tree.

"Well," he said, "I come here to remember the most important day of my life." He paused and then looked down at the kids and said, "Would you like to hear about what happened to me right here in this tree?"

There was no way any of those kids were going to turn down that opportunity.

Our Zacchaeus proceeded to tell the story of how he met Jesus. Every head was tilted back, eyes gazing up, and ears wide open the entire time he spoke.

So, find a tree—it doesn't have to be a Sycamore—and convince some willing soul that he can make a great contribution to children's ministry by dressing up and climbing a tree!

SKIT 2 - Jonah and the Big Fish (Jonah 1 and 2)

DIRECTOR'S NOTES:

Keep your eyes and ears open to what is going on in the community. I once heard of a high school science teacher who made a 90-foot inflatable whale out of heavy black plastic to help his students get a for-real idea of how big a whale might be. Using one regular-size window fan, it could be inflated in about three minutes. I filed away this information until one summer when we included the story of Jonah in our Bible School. I contacted the teacher and he was very willing to let us borrow the gigantic fish.

Once inflated, there was room for at least 40 children inside. We learned a lot that year. As with everything, you take note of things that happen, to keep from making the same mistake again. The black plastic panels of the whale were held together with black duct tape. After being inflated in the hot summer sun for several hours, the duct tape began to melt and come loose. Our whale had several blowholes and was losing air!

DECORATED ROOM

Do you have a room at your church that's not being used at the moment? Decorate the inside of the room to go along with your story, theme for the day or unit. Keep it off limits to the kids, with the doors closed and windows covered until it is time to present the story. If you're using the room for an entire unit, the kids will look forward to visiting that special place.

CLUBHOUSE

For one unit we were starting, we decided it would be fun to tell the story in a clubhouse each week. Because there was an empty room right off our normal meeting place, one of the moms painted the entire room brown. Then, with a little highlighting, she sketched in wooden planks to make it look like a real clubhouse. Add some out-of-alignment windows and signs that looked like a child had written them and the clubhouse was a big hit. The cost of one cheap can of paint enabled us to create a great alternate environment for the kids.

SKIT 3 - Jesus Rides into Jerusalem (Matthew 21:1-11; Mark 11:1-11; Luke 19:29-40; John 12:12-19)

DIRECTOR'S NOTES:

The week we were taking a close look at Jesus entering Jerusalem, the kids were really surprised when they came through the doors. Palm trees made out of carpet rolls and ferns lined a plastic grey runner that made its way through the big room. With all these decorations it didn't seem like the same room they had worshiped in the week before. The setting encouraged their imaginations to transport them somewhere completely different and their curiosity was awakened. One of the children was chosen to portray Jesus and as he passed we waved branches, laid down coats and sweaters, and threw confetti. We also had a couple of kids covered with grey sheets who were pretending to be rocks. Even our rocks shouted hosanna to the King!

SKIT 4 - Solomon Builds the Temple (1 Kings 5 and 6)

DIRECTOR'S NOTES:

Take a Field Trip

If it's not too far, pile the kids in the church van and go offsite for the story. We just happen to be in the middle of a building project and the church is going to be relocating. During that time, one of the stories was about Solomon building the temple. Scripture tells us how it was built and where special items were placed. So we contacted the parents and loaded the kids for a field trip to our building site. We brought along the Ark of the Covenant that the kids had built the week before and placed it at what would be the front of our sanctuary. It was an exciting morning and the kids could definitely connect the Old Testament scripture to their present world. More than likely, you're not in a building project, but you could obtain permission to take them to some building site.

Do you know a place where there's a grassy hillside? Take the kids to that place when you want to tell them the story of Jesus preaching the **Sermon on the Mount (Matthew 5—7; Luke 6:17-49)** or when the crowd was fed by a **Young Boy's Lunch (Matthew 14:13-23; Mark 6:30-46; Luke 9:10-17; John 6:1-15)**.

CHANGE ENVIRONMENTS FOR THESE OTHER STORIES:

- Abram's Tent Home
  (Genesis 15—17) – Create a huge tent that all the kids can get inside at once.

- Baby Moses in the Basket (Exodus 1:1—2:10) – create the river scene with cattails, tall grasses and a large covered basket.

- Crossing the Red Sea (Exodus 13:20—15:21) – Make two high walls of blue plastic that the kids will have to run between. Or, if you can be outside, set up two rows of sprinklers that the kids will run through. Face the sprinklers away from the kids so they won't get wet as they pass through. (But be prepared—the kids will want to get wet!)

- Any of the battles in the Bible – drape camouflage netting across the ceiling and down the walls so the kids feel like they're inside a tent on the battlefield.

- Mary Magdalene Goes to the Garden (John 20:11-18) – create a garden scene with flowers, plants, large rocks (fake) and a bench.

- Jesus Healed the Cripple (John 5:1-18) – Lay a round blue plastic tablecloth in the center of the room to be the Pool of Bethesda. Around it place bath towels, up close and back further, but definitely focused around the pool. Each child will sit on a bath towel (their mat). Pool noodles can be made into arches and the children can hold the ends to the floor. If you have access to a garden arch, it would be a great way to welcome the children into the room.

COSTUMED CHARACTERS

DIRECTOR'S NOTES:

Kids love dress-up, and not just when they're doing the dressing up. Even though they know who is in the costume, it is incredible how they still totally relate to that person as the character. If you are the primary storyteller, then dressing up as a unique character is like inviting a guest to appear and tell the story. It's like having another person there!

There are some special elements that the costumed character needs to keep in mind during preparation and time with the children.

- When an unusual character appears in front of the children, he or she will need a little time to warm up to the personality of the character (unless it is one who appears regularly).

- In addition to a costume, a different voice for that character is just as important as the clothing. Consider voice characteristics such as an accent, speed, volume and/or special character words and phrases as much a part of the character as clothing, props and set.

- If the character uses an accent of some sort, the children should have ample time to get accustomed to the peculiarities of that voice before moving into the story.

Exaggerate characteristics of the character, whether this is a physical element or part of its personality.

- In a way, the character is a walking, talking, breathing cartoon, so study cartoons to see how features are overstated.

- One way to exaggerate physical or personality characteristics is through repetition. If the character is portrayed as clumsy, then he or she should repeatedly trip over objects or drop things. If he or she is easily confused, then the character questions everything and gets disoriented on every possible occasion.

Develop your character completely before it appears for the first time. Once this is done, you've given yourself many more options as far as scripts are concerned for that character. Some questions to answer about the character, and you could definitely come up with more, might be:

- What is the character's full name?

- Who does the character's family include and what is the relationship with each one?

- What business is the character in?

- What is his or her favorite food?

- What is his favorite thing to do?

- Who are his friends and what are they like?

- Does he have a sidekick?

- What is the character's weakness?

- What is the character's strength?

- What angers the character?

- Does the character have a pet?

- Does he have a prominent physical characteristic? If so, what is it?

- What two emotions would you expect this character to display easily?

- Is there something he fears, and if so, what is it?

In a nutshell, what you want to do is interview your character before he or she even exists and then create the character to fit that interview.

Exaggerate, Exaggerate, Exaggerate!

Exaggerate your motions, throwing your arms out to your sides as far as they will go to indicate "big." Stretch as far as you can to reach something on your tippy-toes when you say "high," or pretend to throw a ball by winding up—round and round and round. Exaggerate the inflection in your voice. Sad becomes super sad, in the pit of despair. Excited becomes squeals and high pitches. Quiet is a mouse voice and loud means become a human megaphone. And, exaggerate your props. Whenever you have a choice between props to use, the general rule is to choose the larger one—it shows up better in a large group and if it's an important prop, its size will show just how important it is.

Sometimes the character lends itself to the type of stories he or she tells. I'll describe some of the characters I use for storytelling. Some have personalities or characteristics that definitely lend themselves to a specific type of story. Others, though, are just unusual characters that appear in order to capture the attention of the kids.

CAST MEMBER 1: Winnie Wang

- Creation (Genesis 1:1—2:24)

- Adam and Eve Sin Against God (Genesis 2:8—3:4)

- Jesus Prays in the Garden of Gethsemane (Matthew 26:36-46, Luke 22:39-53, John 18:1-11)

DIRECTOR'S NOTES:

Winnie is a soft-spoken oriental woman who wears a beautiful kimono.

Her words are somewhat broken, imitating someone who speaks English as a second language.

She walks in very short steps, keeping her head slightly down in respect, and her hands tucked in the sleeves of her kimono.

Because she loves to work in her garden, she is especially fond of telling stories about creation and what happened in the Garden of Eden.

The Word of God is very precious to her and everything she says comes back to the Bible.

You can't imagine Winnie becoming angry or raising her voice. Even if she said "Boo!" it would be in a very timid-sounding voice.

You can, however, imagine her being touched so deeply that she would tear up, either because something makes her extremely happy or sad. Her heart can be broken easily.

It's also difficult to imagine that Winnie would have any enemies because she is so willing to serve anyone around her.

At first glance Winnie's costume appears very extravagant. In actuality, it is made from a very simple pattern found in all the common sewing pattern books. And embossed silk (or other shiny slick material) is easy to find.

Because a kimono is a wrap-around garment, it can fit many sizes. The obi (belt) can be made extra long and fastened with Velcro so that it also becomes a one-size-fits-all item.

CAST MEMBER 2: Chef Bakesalot

- Passover (Exodus 12:1-30)

- Manna for Hungry People (Exodus 16)

- Building the Tabernacle (Exodus 25—29)

- Noah (Genesis 6:1—9:17)

- Thrown in a Fiery Furnace (Daniel 3)

DIRECTOR'S NOTES:

When you think of Chef Bakesalot, get a picture of Julia Child in your head.

She has an irritatingly loud broken voice, but is very jolly and fun to be around.

She's very good at laughing at herself, and it's a good thing, because she's constantly doing quirky things that end up causing an upheaval in her kitchen.

Chef Bakesalot is a TV cooking show celebrity and most often appears while filming one of her shows.

She always starts off by asking everyone to turn and wave at the camera in the upper corner of the room (which really isn't there, but the kids always wave anyway).

Occasionally she mentions her husband who is her guinea pig, and she tries all her new recipes on him.

Even though she has been a chef most of her life, she's never quite mastered the art of cracking an egg and oftentimes will get so frustrated with it that she opts to include the shell "to add a little crunchiness."

She loves her chocolate, and anytime she's given the opportunity, will dip whatever food she's working with in chocolate.

The only people she ever gets short with are the camera crew and that's always because she's made a mistake and they haven't gone to a commercial quick enough for her.

She's definitely not afraid of a mess and it's a good thing, because she makes plenty of them.

Even through her loud voice, you are very aware that she cares deeply for everyone in her audience.

Chef Bakesalot wears a very simple costume, and you can actually turn your back to the kids while you put it on (if logistics are difficult).

She wears a bibbed white canvas apron with pockets that have a few long-handled spoons or spatulas sticking out of them.

She never goes anywhere without her chef's hat.

Both these items can be purchased through a kitchen/bulk food supply store (such as GFS) and disposable paper chef hats can be found online at novelty companies.

When talking about the Passover meal and the significance of each item, Chef Bakesalot loves to make an appearance.

In addition to pointing out the significance of each item in the Passover meal, she leads the children in making some haroseth.

PASSOVER MEAL:

Lamb is a reminder of the blood of the lamb that was painted over the door of each Israelite family so that the angel of death would pass over their home.

Bread is made with no yeast because God told the Israelites to get ready for their journey in a hurry. They didn't have time to wait for the bread to rise.

Bitter herbs (which you can show as horseradish) have an awful taste. It must have been terrible to be a slave to the Egyptians.

If you taste your tears you'll realize they are salty. Green herbs dipped in saltwater represent the many tears the Israelites cried because they were held as slaves.

Haroseth is made of several different things and is something like a chutney or salsa. The Egyptians made the Israelite slaves mix together mud, clay, straw and water to make the bricks that would build their magnificent cities. The haroseth would remind them of the bricks and mortar they prepared as slaves.

RECIPE FOR HAROSETH

4 large apples, peeled

1 t lemon juice

1 c finely chopped pecans

4 T brown sugar

2 T honey

1 t cinnamon

½ c raisins

Cut everything into very small pieces. Once the apples are diced, pour the lemon juice over them. Then, mix all the ingredients together in a large bowl. There's no cooking or waiting involved. I find that these ingredients are so familiar to the kids that they are very willing to try this new food, and actually like it.

DIRECTOR'S NOTES:

Chef Bakesalot is a good character to talk about the procedures God gave the Israelites when they were building the tabernacle. There were very specific instructions they were to follow, with specific measurements. This also happened when Noah was building the ark.

Without those instructions the ark would not have held all the cargo of animals and been able to float.

Join the chef in the kitchen as she is about to bake a cake.

First of all, she can't find the recipe, so she decides to wing it and go from memory.

Add the wrong measurement of an ingredient that the children will definitely know is incorrect, such as a cup of salt, instead of a teaspoon.

Chef Bakesalot tries to remember which it was, but decides more is always better so she adds the cup of salt.

True to her abilities, she gets frustrated with breaking the egg and opts to toss the entire thing into the batter, claiming, "It will add a little unexpected crunch which everyone will enjoy."

Using a Mixmaster™ works best, so the ingredients can be mixed even as she adds to the recipe. Of course, the cake is a total failure.

Chef Bakesalot relates the importance of her recipe and the outcome of her cake to the importance of the Israelites' following God's instructions in building the tabernacle or Noah building the ark.

Chef Bakesalot can also be used to tell the story of the three Hebrew children thrown into the fiery furnace and relate that to what happened when she had her oven turned up too high. She can even bring in a charred dish and show it to the children.

CAST MEMBER 3:
Betty Chickencoop

- The Prodigal Son (Eating with the Pigs) - (Luke 15:11-32)

- Peter Denies Christ (A Rooster Gives a Special Wake-up Call) - (Matthew 25:31-75, Mark 14:27-72; Luke 22:31-62; John 18:15-27)

- Moses and the Plagues (Here a Frog, There a Frog, Everywhere a Frog-Frog) – (Exodus 7:14—10:29)

- Balaam's Donkey (Talk to the Animals) – Numbers 22:1-35

- Jacob's Ladder Dream (What's in the Heavens?) – Genesis 27:42—29:12

- The Twelve Spies (An Enormous Grape Crop) – Numbers 13—14

- The Sun and the Moon Stand Still – Joshua 10—12

- Ruth Gleans the Grain – Ruth 1:1—4:17

- The Sower – Matthew 13:1-23; Mark 4:1-20

DIRECTOR'S NOTES:

Betty Chickencoop is a farmer's wife. This character could just as easily be Farmer Chickencoop.

She wears a farm dress and maybe a kitchen apron that you might see your great-grandmother wearing—you know the kind I mean, with the small cotton print and the smell of fried chicken and apple pie that just won't come out.

Betty is usually carrying a bushel basket.

She does her storytelling from a front porch rocking chair or from her garden. A garden can be made by laying down a foam egg crate mattress. (These are mattress overlays the hospital uses to make the

bed softer for patients. They come in several thicknesses; they're flat on the bottom and bumpy on the top, resembling the inside of an egg carton.)

Cover the egg crate with dark burlap and place some artificial vegetables in the rows that are created from the bumps in the foam. Seed packets on the ends of paint stir sticks or tongue depressors can be pushed down in the foam to mark the rows and you have a sweet little garden as a storytelling vignette.

Betty has four children—three are just as sweet as pie, but one son just has a mind of his own.

He's the one who is a challenge to her. She raises her children with a firm, loving hand, and is delighted by the smallest things they do.

It's not uncommon for Betty to talk to the animals that live on the farm, and tell the audience what they've said to her.

One of her favorite things is sitting on her porch after the sun has gone down; she listens to the crickets and bullfrogs, while gazing into the heavens at the stars.

CAST MEMBER 4:
Dr. Fran Bunsenburner
(mysterious things happen)

DIRECTOR'S NOTES:

Dr. Bunsenburner is a zany scientist who is reminded of Bible stories and scripture by what she experiences in her laboratory.

This character uses a German accent (at least as much as possible), so be careful to continue the accent as long as the costume is on.

The costume is very simple: a lab coat, some wide-rimmed glasses, and a crazy wig. As with all the costumes, these are just suggestions, so feel free to add your own touches.

The doctor has two lab assistants: Butane and Petri. They are notorious for causing messes in the lab and for not following instructions.

About the only time Dr. Bunsenburner gets agitated is when these two have gone against the laboratory rules; otherwise, she laughs at herself and the unexpected results she's gotten from her experiments.

As far as favorite foods are concerned, she likes fried pickles (as you'll understand in a moment) and anything that can be warmed over a Bunsen burner.

Dr. Bunsenburner is constantly amazed at how incredibly complicated and inter-related the world that God created is, and she's very insistent that it is because of her faith in God that she enjoys her laboratory so much.

There's always more to discover and understand!

SKIT 1 - Moses and the Burning Bush (Exodus 3—4)

The experiment that Dr. Bunsenburner uses to introduce this story is called "The Glowing Pickle."

PROPS:

- 2 16-penny nails
- A wood plank
- Electrician's tape
- Large dill pickle
- Sharp knife
- Short extension cord

SCENE 1:

Do not tell the children that you are going to be making a pickle light up because the initial part of their discussion will be about what they thought was going to happen.

Cut off the end of the extension cord that does not have the plug on it. Slice through the plastic covering and separate the two wires about 6." Peel back the plastic coating to expose about 1" of both wires.

Wrap each exposed wire around the head of a 16-penny nail. Then, completely cover the exposed wires with electrician's tape.

Insert a nail into each end of the pickle. The nails should not touch one another inside the pickle. From this point on, **do not touch the metal of the nail.** You could experience more of this experiment than you want to!

Lay the pickle on a wood plank (or any nonmetal surface).

Plug the extension cord into a socket and turn out the lights.

Wait a few seconds and you'll notice that the pickle is sizzling and glowing!

SCENE 2: Ask the children:

Did you expect the pickle to light up?

Did you think it would burn?

The Bible tells us about a man who witnessed something that he couldn't believe was happening. He saw one lone bush on fire and it didn't burn up!

DIRECTOR'S NOTES:

Continue telling the story, occasionally referring to the pickle and what happened in the experiment. The experiment got the kids' attention and now they are ready to hear what else the character has to say.

SKIT 2 - Elijah and the Little Cloud (1 Kings 18:41-46)

DIRECTOR'S NOTES:

- Let Dr. Bunsenburner tell this story, but when it comes to the part where the servant spots a tiny little cloud in the distance, move to the experiment.

- Dr. Bunsenburner can say something like, *"Oh my, I know what's going to happen and it makes me think about a wonderful experiment I do in my laboratory!"*

PROPS:

- Bar of Ivory soap
- Large paper plate
- Microwave oven

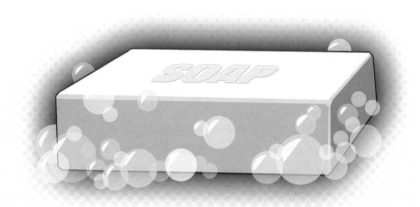

SCENE 1:

DIRECTOR'S NOTES:

This is an amazing experiment, so gather around the microwave and don't blink! Make sure an adult is performing the experiment and the kids are observers.

Not just any soap will work; you need Ivory™.

Unwrap one bar of Ivory™ soap and place it in the center of a large sturdy paper plate. Put the plate in the center of the microwave oven and cook on HIGH for about 2 minutes. Within 10 seconds you'll start to see things change. Be careful not to leave it in the oven too long. If the soap starts touching the sides of the microwave, you'll want to stop. You don't enjoy popcorn that's been overcooked, and you certainly don't want to burn your soap!

Remove it from the microwave and let it cool for a minute.

You've created an amazing soapy cloud!

SCENE 2:

What do you expect the soap to feel like now? After guessing, let the children gently touch the soap. *Were you surprised?*

In its new form, what does it remind you of? (a cloud)

Break off a piece and see if it still works like soap. Even though we wouldn't think it was a bar of soap if we saw it sitting on the counter, it does exactly what we expect soap to do.

What happened as the bar of soap heated up in the microwave?

SCENE 3:

Now, continue on with the story.

Just like our Ivory™ soap bar got bigger and bigger and started looking like a big cloud, so did the little cloud that the servant spotted rising out of the sea.

It wasn't long until the little cloud became a great storm, which ended the draught.

More experiments like these can be found in Beakers, Bubbles and the Bible by this author and available from Warner Press.

CAST MEMBER 4: Captain Kid

PROPS:

- Captain Kid is a pirate who has a parrot sidekick named Crackers.

- Crackers is a parrot puppet who uses a large barrel as a puppet stage.

- You can get an idea of the costume possibilities from the illustration.

- The vest and shirt were made from a pattern found in one of the common pattern books.

- Regular black pants can be worn or leggings.

- Black spats that cover the lower leg and the top of your shoes can be purchased from an online novelty supplier, as well as an assortment of pirate hats.

- The jewelry is just anything gaudy that can be found in your grandmother's jewelry box, although the large medallion is actually an ornament for the Christmas tree.

DIRECTOR'S NOTES:

The captain is a high-spirited pirate who loves the excitement of wandering the seas, but would never do anything to intentionally harm anyone.

Hence, we have a good-hearted pirate, if there be such a thing.

It's easy to find web sites that have full vocabularies along with the meanings of the words befitting a pirate. These are a lot of fun to interject into Captain Kid's speech.

Another interesting feature is that Crackers is constantly finding bottles either floating in the sea or hidden in the clutter of the ship that contain secret messages. These messages often lead the captain into a Bible story.

Captain Kid appears fearless, although Crackers is consumed by fear. When the captain is telling a Bible story Crackers often interrupts because he is scared of what might happen. This repeatedly gives the captain opportunities to assure Crackers and the kids that God is in control.

One recurring prop is a large travel trunk, like you would see in pirate movies, filled with gold and jewels. The trunk provides a place to keep the things important to Captain Kid, like his Bible, a photo of his family and anything else that might be important to the telling of the story.

It's pretty obvious that stories set in the sea or on the seashore would be great opportunities for Captain Kid to appear.

Also, the stories he tells often involve the mention of treasure. Some of these are:

- Crossing the Red Sea (Exodus 13:20—15:21)

- Paul Shipwrecked (Acts 27)

- Store Up Treasure in Heaven (Matthew 6:19-21)

- A Rich Man Came to Jesus (Matthew 19:16-30; Mark 10:17-31)

- Solomon's Special Gift (1 Kings 3—4)

- Simon Tries to Make a Special Purchase (Acts 8:4-25)

ADDITIONAL CAST MEMBERS FOR YOU TO ADD:

CONSTRUCTION WORKER (NAMED CONNIE STRUCTION, BITSY DRILL, CORD SANDERS OR LATHE SANDERS)

- This character could tell stories such as Nehemiah Builds the Wall, Joshua Builds the Altar, or Tower of Babel.

GAME SHOW HOST (NAMED VANNA WRIGHT)

- This character could tell stories that have a big word or phrase in them that the kids have to figure out by playing a *Wheel of Fortune* game.

- Dress in a fancy floor-length gown.

- Words or phrases that could be used in the game are: Nebuchadnezzar, Mephibosheth, Go and sin no more.

- Use these key words to lead into the storytelling.

A DOCTOR (NAMED: QUEASY MD, DR. SAWBONES, EARAKE WHEEZY, IVAN COLDANDACOFF)

- The good doctor would marvel at the miracles of Jesus and be a great one to tell the stories of healing.

A RETIRED SCHOOL TEACHER NAMED GERTRUDE FROGBOTTOM.

- She dons a pair of knee-high hose, one that has slipped down around her ankle, and sensible shoes.

- Gaudy jewelry, bright red lipstick that far surpasses her lips, and a hanky nicely tucked inside her dress for easy retrieval are all part of what endears her to the audience.

- She reminisces about students of long ago and their characteristics or antics remind her of Bible stories.

FIRST PERSON

DIRECTOR'S NOTES:

No storytelling technique comes without preparation, and presenting a story in first person is no different. What you want to accomplish by doing a story from a first-person point of view is to "get into the skin" of the character. You become this character. You see and feel what that person may have seen or felt. Your objective is to let the audience see what's happening through the eyes of this character. I love first-person stories and am convinced that I benefit more from them than the audience, since I really have to understand where each person is coming from in order to communicate effectively.

SKIT 1 - Abraham (Genesis 15 —18)

PROPS:

When I did the first-person story of Abraham, I came up with a full costume. I was so completely covered that many of the kids (and adults) never figured out who I was.

Surprise!

Utilize the element of surprise. Keep your audience off-guard. You can accomplish this in several ways. Don't be afraid to change the volume of your voice unexpectedly. Turn quickly to come face to face with one of the kids. Costumes provide an element of surprise when the kids are expecting you to arrive in your street clothes. They are momentarily taken aback and automatically curious as to what's coming next.

- Look at a picture of a nomad, even a present day nomad in the Middle East, and you will notice that he wears layers of clothing. So, put together biblical garb and think layers.

- Make sure the head is completely covered—that would have protected Abraham from the hot sun.

- Add a large rugged walking stick that is taller than you are.

- Since Abraham is an old man when he's telling this story, purchase a grey beard at a novelty store.

- Now think about the old man, Abraham. How did he appear to others? He more than likely walked slowly, was slightly bent over, and had some gravel in his voice that came with his many years of living.

DIRECTOR'S NOTES:

Abraham should take his time coming out onto the platform. His gate will be the first indicator to the audience that Abraham is really old. His head is down and when he does finally lift it, he's surprised to see the audience.

SCENE 1:

Oh my, what a group we have here. It's so nice to come and share my story with children who want to know more about the One true God, the One who means so much to me, the One who changed my life completely. I almost forgot; I should introduce myself. My name is Abraham. It wasn't always Abraham, though. It used to be Abram, but God changed it along the way. Could I take a few moments and tell you about that?

I had already lived about 100 years when this all happened. My wife, Sarai, was about 10 years behind me, but still as lovely as she was the day we married. (Abraham pauses and acts as though he's reviewing memories in his mind.) *We had everything a couple could ever want—riches, servants, beautiful clothes and wonderfully large tents. We had everything that is, except one thing that was very important to both of us. We had lived our entire lives and never had a child.*

SCENE 2:

Have you ever had a powerful dream? Well, I had a doozy one night. God appeared to me in the dream and told me that Sarai and I were going to have a child—a son. God also told me that this son was a reward for being faithful to Him. That dream shook me up so much I woke up. But God wasn't done speaking with me yet. Even though I was wide awake, God told me to go outside. Quietly, I pulled the flap of the tent door back and walked out into the darkness of the night. God told me to look up, look up at the stars. I leaned back and breathed in the crisp air and gazed upon the most beautiful starlit sky. Then, God asked me if I knew how many stars were in that sky. I started to count them, 1-2-3-4-5, but then realized—I couldn't count the stars—there were too many! That's when God told me He would bless me with so many ancestors that they would number like the stars in the sky. There would be so many they could not be counted. That puzzled me since Sarai and I were both so old and we had never started a family. But I believed the promise God gave me that night. God had always been faithful to me, and I promised to be faithful to Him. I believed; yes, I believed.

That promise was so special that God changed my name. He said I would no longer be called Abram. He gave me a new name, Abraham, which means "father of many." God also changed my sweet Sarai's name to Sarah, which means "princess." Ah yes, she's always been my princess. So, we left our old names and took these new names. Each time someone called me by that new name I was reminded of the promise God made.

Days, weeks, months passed and one day I was sitting outside our tent when I saw three strangers coming. I went out to meet them and invited them to stay with us. I sent for water to wash their feet because they were dusty from their long trip. They were surely hungry, so I told Sarah to make some barley cakes while I cooked some meat for them.

While they were eating one of the men looked up at me and asked, "Where's Sarah?" I told him that she was inside the tent. And then, what the stranger said next startled me. He said, "Sarah will have a son." Sarah must have heard from inside the tent because we heard her laugh. The stranger asked why she was laughing at what he had said. "Does she think she is too old to have a child? Doesn't she know that nothing is too difficult for God to do?"

When they were done eating I walked with them for a while as they continued on their journey. It was on the walk that I realized these weren't ordinary men. Two of the men *were angels and the other was the Lord Himself. (Abraham's voice tears up.) I couldn't believe I was walking with my precious God. It's a day that I will never forget.*

Nothing is too difficult for God to do. Remember that promise He made to me about having a son? We were old and Sarah laughed at the thought, but we did have a son. Even in our old age we had a son, a wonderful son. We named him Isaac, which, by the way, means "laughter." My, how I love that boy! And I believe that God will keep His promise through Isaac to make my ancestors so many they cannot be counted.

Thanks for letting me share my life with you. God changed my name, but more importantly He changed my life. He made a promise and, as always, God is faithful to keep His promises.

OTHER STORIES THAT WORK WELL AS FIRST PERSON STORIES:

David Spares Saul's Life (1 Samuel 24—25)

Jesus Heals a Withered Hand (Matthew 12:1-15, Mark 2:23—3:6, Luke 6:1-11)

Esther (Esther 1—10)

Mephibosheth Faces David (2 Samuel 4:4 and 9:1-13)

For more skits that use First Person, visit www.warnerpress.org/321.html

DIRECTOR'S NOTES:

The beauty of a guest storyteller is in having a different voice for the children to hear. Week after week they listen to your stories and no matter how many different techniques you use it's still you. Guest storytellers are special simply because they are guests, which makes them a novelty. This is really not so much a technique as it is an option because the guest then chooses what technique he or she will employ to tell the story. Most often it becomes a mixture of costumed character, first person.and an environment change.

When recruiting someone as a guest storyteller, watch for people who are descriptive and lively. Good storytellers will come to life at a dinner party and capture everyone's attention just describing something that happened in their day. They can make an ordinary event seem remarkable. The one caution flag I would like to wave, though, is your timing. If you want guest storytellers to do a good job, and I'm assuming you do want to set them up for success, then allow them plenty of time to prepare. Don't expect much if you've made a phone call on Saturday evening. Since this is a one-time event, most guests will spend time working on what they will say and adding special touches—if they are given a proper preparation timeframe.

SKIT 1 - Jesus Is Alive! (Matthew 28:1-10)

- Ask a guest storyteller to dress up in biblical clothing to portray Mary.
- She can station herself outside, tending to some flowers or sitting on a bench in a garden-like setting.

- Take the children outside where they will notice her and then move closer when they question what she's doing.

- When asked, the woman can respond by sharing how the garden brings back wonderful memories for her. Then, she can proceed to ask the children if they would like to hear about what happened to her in a very special garden.

SKIT 2 - A Roman Centurion (Matthew 8:5-13, Luke 7:1-10)

- The centurion was a soldier in the army who was in charge of 100 men and expected to serve for at least 25 years. So this man was a life-long soldier.

- Use your search engine to find a photo of a Roman centurion and then duplicate as much as possible what he wore. Your guest will be very impressive when he enters; give the children a few moments to adjust to this unique person being in their midst.

- The guest's voice should be firm most of the time, but not scary. When he speaks of what Jesus did, though, his voice should soften.

- In order for the story to have its fullest meaning, the guest storyteller needs to make clear what he expects of his men when he gives a command. The significance of this story is not just that Jesus performed a miracle by healing the centurion's servant, but it's in the fact that the centurion demonstrated such incredible faith. He was well aware that when he gave a command, whether or not he was there, he expected that command to be carried out. In the same vein, he recognized that Jesus had power over his servant's sickness and why such power existed in this man called Jesus. Whether or not Jesus came into the house, he could heal the servant because Jesus was in command.

- The guest should also make clear that it was not out of arrogance that he chose not to meet Jesus, but it was because he felt unworthy to be in the presence of someone as holy as Jesus.

INTERJECT DIALOGUE

DIRECTOR'S NOTES:

Even though this technique involves two people, it requires little or no rehearsal. Stories that are appropriate for this technique are ones that are mainly about what one person is saying.

- The main storyteller will be telling **about** what happens.

- The main character of the story will actually **speak** the words.

- The main character takes that as his or her cue and states in actual dialogue, what the storyteller has just expressed.

- This technique goes back and forth between traditional storytelling and a mixture of acting and first-person techniques.

SKIT 1 -   John the Baptist (Matthew 3:1-17, Mark 1:3-11, Luke 3:1-22, John 1:15-34)

STORYTELLER: John, Jesus' cousin, went all over Judea preaching. He wore clothes made from camel's hair and ate locusts and wild honey.

JOHN THE BAPTIST: *Oh yum, supper. I love locusts.* (Picks up a jumbo raisin that has been planted as a bug.)

STORYTELLER: He preached that people should turn back to God because the kingdom of heaven would soon be here.

JOHN THE BAPTIST: (Yelling) *"Turn back to God. The kingdom of heaven will soon be here!"*

STORYTELLER: He told the people they needed to repent.

JOHN THE BAPTIST: *"Repent. You all need to repent!"*

STORYTELLER: Many people did turn back to God and John baptized them. Some people wondered who he was and they asked if he was the Christ. John was quick to deny that.

JOHN THE BAPTIST: *"I am not the Christ."*

STORYTELLER: Then they asked if he was Elijah and he denied that also.

JOHN THE BAPTIST: *"I am not Elijah."*

STORYTELLER: They asked if he was a prophet and he said that he wasn't.

JOHN THE BAPTIST: *"I am not a prophet."*

STORYTELLER: The religious men wanted to know who he was. When they asked, he told them he was the voice that cried out in the wilderness to make way for the Lord.

Word Play

Use age-appropriate vocabulary, but don't be afraid to present the kids with one new word now and then that will challenge them. Make sure you put it into context where they can tell what it means by the words used in the rest of the sentence. If every sentence is complex and full of words from a college textbook, then you'll lose your audience. In the same light, if you simplify the language too much, kids will tune out because they feel like they're involved in something really meant for much younger children.

JOHN THE BAPTIST:	*"I am the voice crying out in the wilderness, 'Make way for the Lord.'"*
STORYTELLER:	The religious men wanted to know why he baptized if he wasn't the Christ, or Elijah or a prophet. He told them he only baptized with water. The one who was coming would baptize with the Holy Spirit.
JOHN THE BAPTIST:	*"I only baptize with water. The one who is coming will baptize with the Holy Spirit."*
STORYTELLER:	John was humbled. He told the men that he was not even worthy to untie the sandals of the great one who was coming.
JOHN THE BAPTIST:	*"I am not even worthy to untie the sandals of the one who is coming."*
STORYTELLER	When Jesus was about 30 years old, He went to the Jordan River to find John, for He wanted to be baptized. When John saw Jesus coming he pointed to Jesus and called out that He was the Lamb of God. He told the people, "This is the One who will take away the sins of the world." Jesus was the One who was much greater than John.
JOHN THE BAPTIST:	*"There He is. Here comes the Lamb of God. Here is the One who will take away the sins of the world. Here is the One who is much greater than I am."*
STORYTELLER:	And then John asked Jesus why He had come out to the desert. John didn't feel worthy to baptize Jesus.
JOHN THE BAPTIST:	*"Why have you come out here? I am not worthy to baptize you."*
STORYTELLER:	Jesus told John that He must be baptized because it was part of God's plan. So John took Jesus out into the Jordan River and baptized Him. When Jesus came up out of the water the sky opened up and the Spirit of God came down from heaven like a dove and rested on Jesus. Then a voice from heaven said, "This is my son and I am very pleased with him."

OTHER STORIES APPROPRIATE TO USE WITH THE INTERJECT DIALOGUE TECHNIQUE:

- An Angel Visits Daniel (Daniel 7—11) – interject dialogue of the angel

- Ezra Teaches (Ezra 7—10 and Nehemiah 8) – interject dialogue of Ezra

- Paul Preaches on Mars Hill (Acts 17:16-34) – interject dialogue of Paul

- Deborah Leads Israel (Judges 4 —5) – interject dialogue of Deborah

DIRECTOR'S NOTES:

As you analyze a story and review what you have to work with, it's helpful to list the nouns that have a place in the story. Many times these can be made into props or positioned as part of the scenery. On some occasions, though, you find a story that has one particular item that stands out. It shines. It asks to be noticed. This item is either mentioned repeatedly throughout the story or has some great significance to what is taking place in the story. In some instances it may even be an additional character.

Once this outstanding prop has been identified, determine how it's going to be used.

- Is it going to sit in the room and every time it's mentioned in the story, the storyteller moves close to it?

- Will the storyteller hold it the entire time?

- Is it something that each child should have to interact with during the story?

- Or, will this special prop be brought into the room in the middle of the story for bigger impact?

Let's look at a few examples of how the one powerful prop technique can be used.

SCRIPT 1 - The Woman at the Well (John 4:1-43)

DIRECTOR'S NOTES:

In this story the **significant prop is a well**. A well can be made in a variety of ways.

- Gather rocks from a stream and stack them to form something that resembles a well. That's a lot of heavy carrying though.

- I like to use a large cardboard box like a lawn mower would come in. Completely remove the top of the box. Then, cover the outside of the box with a paper that has stone printed on it. This can usually be purchased at a teacher's supply store or through prom suppliers, such as www.stumpsprom.com (from the home page, click on Backgrounds).

- Or, the box can be painted to look like stacked stones. To do this, give the box a base coat that will actually end up being the mortar between the stones. I like to use a stencil made from some poster board to determine the stones. Hold the stencil up to the box and dab different shades of grays in the space with a sponge. When the stencil is removed, you're left with something that looks very much like a stone. Reposition the stencil so a little space is left between it and the last stone painted, and sponge paint another one. Continue doing this until the box is covered.

- We've even put a galvanized tub down in the cardboard well and filled it with blue Kool-Aid. When the story is over the kids can draw out their own drink from the well.

What follows is a condensed story with many scenes provided to point out how the **well** is important to this story. When you actually tell the story, you'll give more details about each one of these scenes.

- When Jesus was tired He sat down at a **well** that Jacob had dug generations before. He waited there while His disciples went on ahead to purchase food.

- A Samaritan woman came to get water at the **well.** She saw the Jewish man sitting there but did not approach Him.

- Jesus asked the woman to give Him a drink from the **well.**

- The woman questioned Jesus as to why He, a Jew, would ask a Samaritan woman for a drink. His reply was strange and puzzled her. Jesus said that if she knew who was asking her for a drink, she would ask Him for living water.

- The woman was still confused because Jesus did not have anything with which to draw water from the **well**. How would He give her living water?

- Jesus tried to explain to her that those who drank from this **well** would get thirsty again. But, if they drank of the living water that He could give, they would never be thirsty again. The living water He spoke of brings eternal life. Jesus went on to tell her that He was the one they were looking for—the long-expected Messiah.

- When the woman heard this, she left her jar at the **well** and went into the city to tell everyone about the amazing stranger she had met.

- They were so interested that they too went to the **well** to hear what Jesus had to say. His words touched their hearts and their minds, and they asked Him to stay for several more days so they could hear more.

DIRECTOR'S NOTES:

In this story, the **well** is mentioned in each of these scenes. It is for different reasons, but each time the well has importance. It is a meeting place, a provider of a valuable resource, and the subject of an object lesson that Jesus used to teach.

Now, consider using a character as a prop. I see that questioning look on your face, but before you throw this idea out, let me give you an example.

SCRIPT 2 - Lazarus, Come Forth (John 11:1-54)

DIRECTOR'S NOTES:

In preparation for this story, enlist someone to be the **prop character**—**Lazarus**. The main character of the story actually becomes the prop.

- He is not seen until near the end of the story, so his presence is unnecessary until that time.

- His costume is unique in that he will be wrapped in grave clothes.

- A teenage boy is perfect for this and will actually jump at the opportunity. Rip a couple of old sheets in strips that are about 6" wide; these sheets should be light in color and without print.

- As a base, the character prop should wear a white t-shirt and light-colored pants or shorts, along with white socks.

- Wrap the sheeting strips around the young man, securing the ends to one another by using stick-on Velcro® dots.

Teenagers that I had in junior church as second graders can still recall the day when I used this storytelling technique. It made a lasting impression on them, and they can still tell you what happened in John 11:1-54.

SCENE 1:

- The storyteller will begin this story by telling the first section with as much inflection and emotion as possible, using a traditional storytelling style.

- The Lazarus prop will be stationed right outside a door that is slightly cracked open. (Having helpers with Lazarus is always a good idea, so they can listen for cues and help if there is a costuming problem.)

- When the storyteller comes to the part where Jesus calls to Lazarus, the storyteller should use a booming voice and say, *"Lazarus, come forth!"*

- If the storyteller has been animated in the first part of the story this won't seem too unusual, until the children witness what happens.

- *"Come forth"* is the character prop's cue to enter the room.

- The door swings open and Lazarus, in his grave clothes, comes into the room, either hopping or walking (depending on how he has been wrapped).

- Pause for the children to react and take it in.

SCENE 2:

- In the next part of the story Jesus tells the people to unwrap Lazarus because he isn't dead.

- Direct the children to do the same to the Lazarus character prop. They can approach him and pull the grave clothes from him.

DIRECTOR'S NOTES:

There is nothing scary about the way this story is presented if you don't make it scary. In the biblical account there is hesitation on the onlookers' part because the body has been in the tomb for several days, and there is overwhelming surprise. They then react the way anyone would when they have witnessed an incredible miracle. Parallel your storytelling to these biblical reactions and you'll give the children an experience that will bond them with the biblical account. Believe me, you'll have kids talking about what they did at church when this technique is used!

SKIT 3 - The Writing on the Wall (Daniel 5)

PROPS:

- The one powerful prop for this story is an item called a *WavyWand*. This is a special wand that projects words in mid-air when you wave it. They run approximately $30 and can be purchased from several different websites, including www.wavywand.com.

- For this story you'll want to program the words **"Mene-Tekel-Upharsin"** according to the instructions on the package. The words on the wall were actually "Mene, Mene, Tekel, Upharsin," but you can only put 20 characters in the *WavyWand* at a time and there are no commas on the wand.

DIRECTOR'S NOTES:

- Position someone behind a table that is draped with a floor-length tablecloth. This person will be ready to use the *WavyWand* when the time is right.

- Dim the lights when you're ready to tell the story. The kids will wonder why it's a little dark but don't let on what's about to happen.

- You can say, *"In the middle of a party that King Belshazzar was giving, something very strange happened."*

- This is the cue for the person controlling the *WavyWand* to project the words on the wall. (You do this by waving the wand back and forth with lots of wrist action. Practice beforehand in a mirror so you can get a feel for how fast your hand must move in order to project the words.)

- Leave the words there while the rest of the story is told.

- *None of the wise men could tell King Belshazzar what the words meant, but when Daniel was brought to the King, he told him the meaning of each word. Everything the strange words said came true that very night.*

OTHER STORIES TO USE ONE POWERFUL PROP WITH:

- Jacob's Dream (Genesis 27:42—29:12) – ladder

- Jesus Healed the Cripple (John 5:1-18) - mat

- Mary Anoints Jesus (Matthew 26:6-13, Mark 14:3-9, John 12:1-11) – bottle of perfume

- The Stoning of Stephen (Acts 6:7—8:3) – hand-sized rock

For more Scripts that use One Powerful Prop, visit www.warnerpress.org/321.html

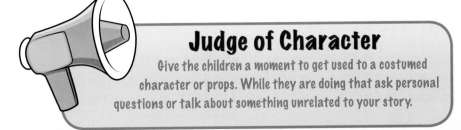

Judge of Character
Give the children a moment to get used to a costumed character or props. While they are doing that ask personal questions or talk about something unrelated to your story.

DIRECTOR'S NOTES:

Unlike many of the other techniques that are somewhat limited by the repetition in the story, items that can become props, or scenes that can be acted out, the **PFFFFT** technique can be used with every story. There won't be a list of additional stories you can use this technique with because it includes everything.

The challenge with this technique, though, is being able to put on paper the pronunciation of "**PFFFFT**." So, here we go; I'll do my best.

- In order to make the **PFFFFT** sound, you must have moist lips.

- Put your lips together and push out a little burst of air. It will make a short buzzing sound that tickles your lips.

- If you happen to have played the trumpet in junior high band, it resembles the way you would have blown into the mouthpiece. Remember how the teacher had you remove the mouthpiece from the trumpet and just blow into that. It wasn't music, but it got your mouth in the right position. Without the mouthpiece you make a **PFFFFT** sound, which is a little less like a duck call than when using the trumpet mouthpiece.

DIRECTOR'S NOTES:

Caution the children that this strange little sound is to be made **only by the storyteller**. The children are not to imitate you or you may find yourself in the middle of a spit spray. If you set guidelines for the children before you make your first **PFFFFT**, they won't be disappointed, because the novelty of the technique will keep their interest. (I know you're all trying it right now as you read, so please set the book aside while you experiment!)

Using **PFFFFT** stories to tell a brand new story that the children have never heard is difficult and risky. The **PFFFFT** storytelling technique operates on the idea that the children are at least familiar with the story and you're refreshing their memories. If using **PFFFFT** to tell a story for the first time, then make sure your gestures are large and specific to help the children figure out what you're talking about.

In preparation for a **PFFFFT** story:

- Identify key words in the story that you will leave out—actually, you're not leaving them out, but replacing them with the **PFFFFT** sound. I like to make a copy of the story as it appears in *Egermeier's Bible Story Book*, and then highlight the words I'm going to target.

- Always rehearse a **PFFFFT** story to get familiar with where you'll be replacing those key words.

- The more you have rehearsed, the faster you'll be able to tell the story. The faster the telling, the more fun the kids will have in trying to keep up with you.

- Before starting the story, make your warm-up exercises elaborate in front of the children.

- Take a drink of water and lick your lips real big. Gargle. Stretch your face.

- Set your stance as if you're going to run a race.

- Once you begin, each time the children hear **PFFFFT**, they are to yell out the word that you have replaced.

- Acknowledge the missing word the children identified by repeating it, but then hop right back into the story and continue on.

- Resist the traditional way of calling on a child for the correct answer. If you do that, you'll break the flow and it becomes no more than a pencil and paper fill-in-the-blank quiz.

- Many times the **PFFFFT** word does not fall at the end of the sentence. Go ahead and say the entire phrase or sentence.

- The kids will go back and fill in what should have been said.

This technique works especially well if you're working through a unit, such as on Moses or Joseph, where you're adding to the story each week. To get everyone caught up and on the same page, **PFFFFT** is a fun way to accomplish that. Or, if you operate on a two-week study of each story, rather than the traditional story-a-week teaching schedule, **PFFFFT** is great to use on the second week.

(If you really can't master the **PFFFFT**, then ring a counter bell, but you severely diminish the effectiveness of the technique if you do that.)

SCRIPT 1 - The Road to Damascus (Acts 9:1-19)

DIRECTOR'S NOTES:

The words in red are the words that you replace with **PFFFFT**.

SCENE 1:

- As a devout Jew, Saul believed strongly in the Law of Moses. He was willing to fight against anyone who questioned that or anyone who believed otherwise. When people started believing in Jesus as the Savior God had sent, Saul was outraged. He hated the followers of Jesus and did his best to get rid of them. He had some put in prison and others he had killed.

- To get away, many of the believers left Jerusalem. When Saul heard there were lots of believers in Damascus, he decided to go there. A few friends went along with Saul to hunt down the Christians.

- Saul was not the only one going to Damascus. When believers in Jerusalem heard what he was doing, they hurried to Damascus to warn them that Saul was coming to arrest them, or maybe even kill them.

SCENE 2:

- Saul and his friends were almost to Damascus when a bright light came down around them. Saul fell to the ground. The men heard something that sounded like thunder, but Saul heard something different. He heard a voice from heaven that said, "Saul, why are you persecuting me?" When Saul asked who the voice was, he heard, "I am Jesus of Nazareth, the one you are against." Saul didn't know what to do, but Jesus told him to go on into Damascus.

SCENE 3:

- Something awful had happened to Saul's _eyes_. He was now _blind._ The men who were with him were fine, but Saul couldn't see. They took Saul into Damascus to the house of Judas. Saul sat there in the blind darkness for _three_ days. He was so frightened and upset that he couldn't _eat_ or _drink_. He now knew that what he had been doing against the _Christians_ was wrong.

SCENE 4:

- There was a believer in Damascus by the name of Ananias. God told _Ananias_ where Saul was and also told Ananias to go find _Saul_. God wanted Ananias to lay his _hands_ on Saul's _eyes_ so that Saul would be able to see. But Ananias had heard of all the horrible things Saul had done to believers. He was _afraid_ of what might happen. God told Ananias that _Saul_ was a chosen servant and that he would do great things for the kingdom of God. Ananias' fears were gone and he went to find Saul.

SCENE 5:

- When Ananias found Saul he said, "The Lord Jesus who met you on the _road_ to Damascus sent me here so your sight could be returned and so you would be filled with the Holy Spirit." Ananias put his _hands_ on Saul's _eyes_ and something like _scales_ fell from his face. Saul could see again! Immediately, he wanted to be _baptized_. He would never go back to the life of chasing down Christians to arrest them. Instead, he would start _preaching_ about Jesus that very day, telling people about how God could change their _lives_, just like God changed his.

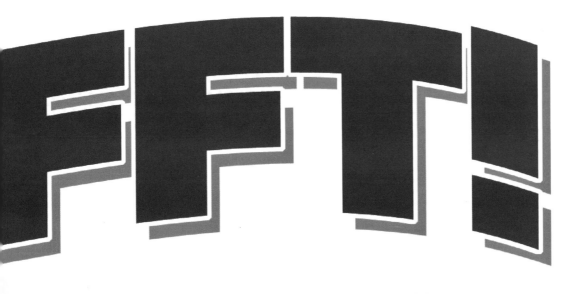

DIRECTOR'S NOTES:

In this storytelling technique you provide something for the children to focus on—something unique that will draw their attention. At the same time, the item needs to be fairly stationery, with very little movement to it. What you're trying to do is give the children something to concentrate on that will help them relax and listen. Physical focal points help eliminate distractions in the room.

SKIT 1 - Focal Point: Post with Drapes of Cloth

(The Woman Who Touched Jesus' Garment, Matthew 9:19-22)

As Jesus and the disciples were going to the official's home, a woman who had had a hemorrhage for twelve years came up behind him. She touched the fringe of his robe, for she thought, "If I can just touch his robe, I will be healed." Jesus turned around and said to her, "Daughter, be encouraged! Your faith has made you well." And the woman was healed at that moment (NLT)*.

PROPS:

- To prepare for telling this story, create a very interesting focal point. A rather large area is needed to do this, so make special arrangements if you need to.

- Construct a self-standing sturdy post from a 4" x 4" piece of wood.

- This post needs to stand about four feet tall.

- Gather at least twelve pieces of cloth that are 3-4 yards long and 20-25" wide. It doesn't matter what patterns these have on them, but lighter weight material works best. Remnants can be purchased at discount department stores for a dollar per yard.

- Use a staple gun to attach one end of each piece of cloth to the top of the post.

- Pull the other end of the cloth out from the post to create a pinwheel effect.

DIRECTOR'S NOTES:

When the children come into the area, instruct them to sit at the ends of the cloth. They should sit back from the cloth where it will take a stretch for them to reach a piece.

- Matthew 9:19-22 tells a very short story, but the desire and faith of the woman mentioned are powerful.

- You will need to describe the setting of a crowd that was pushing in around Jesus. *They wanted to hear everything He had to say and to possibly witness another one of His miracles.*

- *In the middle of this, there was a woman who for twelve years had struggled with a health condition that caused her to bleed continuously.*

- *She was convinced that Jesus could change her life. He could stop the bleeding; He could make her well.*

- *But she couldn't get His attention. There were so many people! She couldn't get close enough to talk to Him. What could she do?*

- Make sure the children feel the desperation of this woman.

- *The woman thought to herself, if I can't get right up to Jesus to talk to Him face-to-face maybe I can touch His garment. Just being able to touch Him would make me well.*

- *The Bible tells us that she reached out and touched the edge of his cloak.* At this point, encourage the children to reach out and grab the end of a piece of cloth lying in front of them. Let them continue to hold the cloth while you finish telling them how Jesus responded.

SKIT 2 - Focal Point: Marshmallow on a Stick

PROPS:

- For each child make a marshmallow on a stick by pushing a large cotton ball onto the end of a stick that you might find in your yard. (Don't use a dowel rod; you want the rustic outdoors feel of a real stick.)

- Also, create a campfire scene. You can do this with some more sticks piled on the floor with scraps of yellow and orange tissue paper tucked down under.

- Then, place a ring of stones around the campfire.

- There's also a fake indoor fire you can purchase that is loads of fun in any weather. You can find it at www.indoorcampfire.com.

DIRECTOR'S NOTES:

The children will sit around the campfire while the story is being told. They can hold their marshmallow on a stick over the fire to roast it and turn it occasionally to get it nice and golden brown. This technique is especially mesmerizing for preschool through first grade. Stories around a campfire always make great memories, but for little ones they can be a little scary. This indoor campfire takes the fear out of the experience and brings the fun indoors.

SKIT 3 - Focal Point: Candle

DIRECTOR'S NOTES:

What do adults use to create a relaxing, quiet evening? Light a candle. How do adults create a quiet prayer service? Light candles. There's something about candles that immediately put us in the frame of mind where we leave stress behind and quiet our spirits. Watching the dancing flames somehow drives away the things that are tangling up our thoughts. It's the same for kids.

PROPS:

- Dim the lights and light a candle and you'll transform a group of high-strung kids into an attentive and quiet audience.

- Candles can be dangerous, and because of that you need to think through the safety rules the children need to understand.

  - The two main rules that we follow are:

    (1) No one blows at the candle, whether they're trying to make it dance or trying to blow it out, unless instructed to do so by the leader, and

    (2) Everyone stays behind a line on the floor.

- If the children gather in a circle around the candle, the sit-behind line can be formed by placing masking tape on the floor a safe distance from the candle.

- Communicate clearly that if anyone decides to test the rules, then the candle will be immediately removed from the story area. No warnings, no second chances.

DIRECTOR'S NOTES:

Think about which stories you would like to hear by candlelight. There are some that just seem to fit well in a hushed setting. Think about using a candle or a campfire as your physical focal point with:

- Who Do You Say that I Am? (Matthew 16:13-28; Mark 8:27—9:1; Luke 9:18-27)

- Paul's Nephew Comes to the Rescue (Acts 23:11-35)

- Elijah Hears a Gentle Whisper (1 Kings 19:9-21)

- An Angel Releases Peter from Prison (Acts 12:1-23)

* Holy Bible, New Living Translation copyright © 1996, 2004. Used by permission of Tyndale House Publishers. All rights reserved.

DIRECTOR'S NOTES:

Kids love viewing PowerPoint stories. Kids love making PowerPoint stories. They're just great fun from every aspect. You can't go wrong when you change up the story by presenting it on PowerPoint slides. And, you're thinking, "Where do you get these PowerPoint slides?" I'm glad you asked. You make them yourself. All it takes is a digital camera, a computer to put it all together, and some characters.

Now, part of the fun of PowerPoint storytelling is deciding what you're going to use as the characters. I have a friend, Ryan Frank, who uses a cast of Mr. Potato Heads to tell his stories. (You can purchase some of those on www.tatertales.com if you'd like.) But, you can also use dolls, puppets, stuffed animals or Lego creations.

Once you've assembled a cast of characters, then you need to break down the story into scenes that can be described in one sentence. Position the characters to act out that scene and then take a picture of them. Take a couple of pictures, just in case you've not held your hand steady. (My husband and I were working with eleven Mr. Potato Heads in putting a PowerPoint story together. We took the characters all apart before downloading the pictures. When we looked at the pictures later, there were four that were blurry. Consequently, we had to put all eleven Mr. Potato Heads back together in exactly the same way we had them before to retake those four photos. Don't make this mistake!) Then, go to the next scene. Set up the characters and take the next picture.

Once you've transferred the pictures to a PowerPoint presentation, it's time to add the narrative. Create a text box to lay over the picture in a place that is fairly blank. This can be in a different place on each slide. In that text box, write the narrative that goes along with that scene. This way, when the slide presentation is shown, the viewer can read it to himself much like a comic book, or a leader can read along as the slides progress. Don't forget to include a slide acknowledging those who participated in creating this masterpiece. Who knows when you might reuse this story and get a little amusement from seeing the names.

STORIES THAT WORK WELL WITH POWERPOINT

- Let Down through the Roof (Matthew 9:2-8, Mark 2:1-12, Luke 5:18-26)

- Crossing the Red Sea (Exodus 13:20—15:21)

- The Ten Lepers (Luke 17:11-19)

- Little Children Are Brought to Jesus (Matthew 19:13-15, Mark 10:13-16)

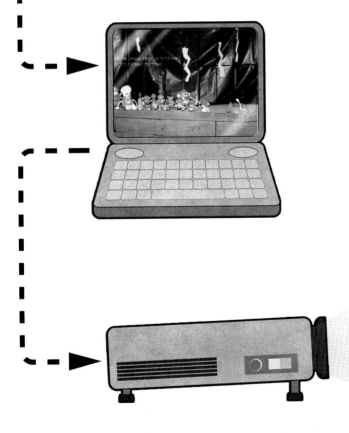

DIRECTOR'S NOTES:

Puppets have been around forever and can be made out of just about anything…from a wooden spoon…to a sock…to a cardboard box…to a sponge. A little imagination is all you need! The wonderful thing is, puppets are timeless. As one of the oldest theatrical traditions, puppetry has been used with children and adults. What have you noticed children do when they are around inanimate objects? Remarkably, they create voices and personalities for their toys, stuffed animals and pets. They've made their own puppets!

Take these two hints and keep the use of puppets lively, fun and beneficial.

1. A storytelling technique, no matter what it is, becomes a poor technique when it is overused.

2. Schedule the puppets to appear often enough to delight the children, but not so often that they become routine. Like the old entertainer's motto says, "Leave 'em wanting more."

REHEARSAL:

- Not everyone makes a good puppeteer, regardless of how simple it may look. Mistakenly, people think they can pick up a puppet at the last minute and pull off a script. That's far from the truth unless they're very experienced. It takes practice and more practice…but it sure is fun!

- Take into account the many tips and techniques to learn if puppets are to be done effectively, and then train your puppeteers.

- Nothing will lose an audience quicker than for a puppet to be talking but not synchronized with the mouth movement. Inexperienced puppeteers will bite down and close the mouth each time a word is said, but just the opposite should be done. The puppet appears to talk when his mouth is open. Not every syllable has to have a mouth movement, but the heavy syllables do.

- A good way to rehearse is to place the puppet in front of a mirror while you talk so you can see what the puppet looks like to the kids.

CAST:

- Two types of people to look for in general are those who are very coordinated and those who can keep a steady beat. Avoid people who are "rhythmically challenged."

- Once you've identified people who will become puppeteers, provide them with training through reading material, training videos, and/or workshops (either ones they can personally attend or ones they can listen to on CD). Even if the workshops are not geared toward teaching the Bible, you'll find the technique training very valuable.

PROPS: HOMEMADE PUPPETS

The best way to increase your cast of puppets is to find a seamstress or a crafty person in your church who will make them for you. Now, before you get overwhelmed and flip out on me, there are patterns. People with sewing talents don't have to create the puppets from scratch. Most of the sewing pattern companies have a variety of puppet patterns in their catalogs.

A basic puppet-person pattern can be turned into any character with a change of clothes, glasses, a different hairstyle, and of course, its own unique voice.

You'll have to check your puppets, but ours wear a child's size 2 clothing, which makes outfitting simpler; we just go to yard sales and watch for appropriate

Frog in the Throat

We have a frog choir—20 green felt frogs that are small enough for children to handle. Each one cost us about a dollar to make. There are ten girls and ten matching boys (color of bow ties and hair bows match), so the frogs can partner if we like. Once the story is told, the kids can retell it to one another by breaking into small groups and using the puppets to talk to one another. Our puppets also love to sing praise songs.

children's clothing.

In addition to human puppets, patterns are available for all kinds of animals.

Puppets can be created out of the strangest materials. Many of these will not have moveable mouths, but they can still be fun.

- **Sock puppets** – forget the white or black sock and look for those bright colors. You can often find a treasure of brightly colored socks at the dollar store because they're not the ones that fly off the shelves.

- **Paper plate puppets** – fold a green paper plate over and make a frog.

- **Wooden spoon puppets** – again, the best place to get a good deal on wooden spoons is at the dollar store. Add some wiggle eyes, yarn hair and some other features, and you've got another way to communicate.

- **Glove puppets** – cut the fingers out of a stretch glove or a garden glove. Add the face and you're in business.

- **Paper sack puppets** – while the sack is flattened, draw the face of a puppet on the bottom flap of the sack but only to the upper lip. The lower lip goes on the side of the bag right where the bottom flap reaches. Place the fingertips down in the bottom flap and the mouth will move.

- **Papier-mâché puppets** – blow up a balloon and cover it with papier-mâché strips. Ears and a nose can be built up with the papier-mâché to give the head more dimension. Once it is dry, pop the balloon and paint the features. A paint stir stick or some other kind of stick can be attached to the hole that was left at the base of the balloon when it was popped.

SPECIALTY PUPPETS

Aside from traditional puppets that talk and possibly have moving arms, there are puppets with special features that make them even more attractive and fun to use.

One such puppet from Amaze Healing Wings (www. amazehealingwings.com) has a patented heart on a string. All of the Amaze Healing Wings puppets have a pocket that holds a heart on a string. This heart can be retrieved during the script. It is actually a pouch that can hold little objects that act as prompters or teasers about the script that follows. The puppet can be asked what he *has on his heart* that day and then the narrator can pull the heart out of the pocket to find its contents.

The puppet is then asked to explain the connection between the object and the issue at hand. This leads into Bible story time where the puppet can be the primary storyteller or he can listen as the leader tells the story.

Here's a wonderful example of a script where a prompting item is in the puppet's heart and the puppeteer tells the story.

I'd like to thank Darcie Maze (www.puppetswithaheart.com) and Kim Star-Voss (www.faithlifeministries.net) for allowing their script to be printed here to model how puppets can be used in telling Bible stories. Both of these women travel worldwide, telling God's stories through puppets and equipping other puppeteers.

SCRIPT 1 - TRUSTING / LION

Object Needed: Place in the heart a small stuffed lion or the picture of a lion.

Theme: Trust in God. Be a trusting friend.

Scripture: Daniel 6:23

"The king was overjoyed and gave orders to lift Daniel out of the den. And when Daniel was lifted from the (lions') den, no wound was found on him, because he had trusted in his God."

(Puppet comes out of bag and whispers in your ear.)

Good day, puppet! You are saying that you want to get rid of something that you are thinking about. You say it is something that you are afraid of. Really?

What is it that scares you, puppet? (Puppet whispers.) *You say that you can't say the words. You are too scared. You keep thinking about something that is scary.*

Actually, if you are thinking about something that makes you afraid, then it might be in your heart. Your heart is who you really are right now. (Puppet whispers.) *Puppet says that right now he really is someone that is afraid.*

All right, my friend. Let's take a look inside your heart. (Check puppet's heart.)

It's a lion (or picture of a lion). *It's a little lion. Is this what you are afraid of, puppet? A lion?*

(Puppet nods head YES and whispers.) *Puppet says he definitely is afraid of a lion. But lions are fun to see in a zoo, puppet. I imagine that many of these children would love to see the lions in a zoo!* (Puppet whispers.) *Puppet says that we TRUST the zoo to keep the animals away from us so we can be safe. We TRUST the zoo for our safety. This is true, puppet. We TRUST that the zoo will keep the animals away from us so we can enjoy them without being afraid that they will come near us.* (Puppet nods head YES.)

This may be a good time to remember a story from the Bible. It's the story about a man named Daniel. Daniel trusted God very much. He prayed to God many times every day. And when the king said that people should stop praying to a god and pray only to the king, Daniel still kept praying to God. One day they took Daniel away and told the king that Daniel was still praying to God, not to the king. So the king had his men throw

Daniel in a cage, or a den of lions.

(Puppet whispers.) *That's right. I would be afraid of those lions too. But Daniel had faith and trusted that God would save him and keep him safe from the lions. And God did just that. He shut the mouths of the lions and they did not hurt Daniel at all. Daniel was in the lions' den all night long and did not get hurt from the lions. The next day when the king saw Daniel, this is what happened. In Daniel 6:23, we read: "The king was overjoyed and gave orders to lift Daniel out of the den. And when Daniel was lifted from the (lions') den, no wound was found on him, because he had trusted in his God."*

(Puppet whispers.) *That's right, my friend. It is so good to trust God because He keeps us safe. So we can use this little lion to remember to trust God. Puppet also wants to learn how to be a trusting friend. We can do that by being as trusting as God wants us to be. Being a true friend who helps others is being someone who can be trusted. We should all trust God. He will help us be a trusting friend to others. Thanks, my friends! Good-bye!*

SPECIALTY PUPPET #2:

- Another special puppet is one that is made of material that glows under a black light.

- When using these puppets, a special stage of solid black must be constructed and the room needs to be light-tight (free from incoming light).

- Puppeteers need to wear dark, solid, long-sleeve clothing to prevent any exposed skin or light clothing from glowing in the dark also.

- Props should be made out of glow-in-the-dark materials to compliment the puppet.

- Use your computer search engine to find sites where these special puppets can be purchased. One of the sites I prefer is www.puppetrevelation.com, because they have a variety of human black light puppets, fish, flowers and cute hairy monsters.

Another website, www.onewaystreet.com, sells a black light puppet called a Stretch-A-Belly puppet. One hand is used to hold the foot control bar, and the other hand is used to manipulate the mouth. They jump, dance and stretch, unlike other puppets.

PARALLELING THE STORY

Sometimes puppets are fun to use to parallel a Bible story, using different characters, but keeping a similar story line and main point. The following script does not tell the story, but is great for reinforcing the point. It's an excellent exercise to ask the children to draw parallels between what the puppet said and did to what happened in the Bible story. This script also shows how one character can be portrayed by a puppet or by a person standing outside the puppet stage. In this instance, Farmer Chickencoop could be a puppet or a live person.

The Real Deal

Always communicate with the kids that the stories you are telling them are from the Bible-about real people who knew God-not fairytales. Through the stories in the Bible we can understand how God touches our lives. God speaks to us through these stories.

THE PRODIGAL SON

PUPPET SCRIPT

Farmer Chickencoop:	*Hey boys and girls, would you like to meet one of my special animal friends here on the farm? Let's see if I can find her. Her name is Hennah. Could you help me call her? Hennah, oh Hennah!*
Hennah:	*Cluck-cluck-cluck.* (Throw some feathers in the air as she appears, squawking.)
Farmer C:	*Boys and girls, say hello to Hennah, one of the chickens on my farm. Hello, Hennah.*
Hennah:	*Good-bye.*
Farmer C:	*No, Hennah, say hello.*
Hennah:	(Singing) *You say hello, but I say good-bye.*
Farmer C:	*Good-bye?*
Hennah:	*Yeah, good-bye.*
Farmer C:	*You must be confused, Hennah. When you meet someone, you say hello.*
Hennah:	*Not if you're leaving.*
Farmer C:	*Excuse me, boys and girls. I think I need to talk to Hennah a minute.* (Turns to puppet.) *What do you mean, leaving?*
Hennah:	*I'm leaving. I'm leaving the farm. Yep, this is the day. I'm going to walk down the path, out the gate, and start down that big exciting road out there.*
Farmer C:	*Why would you want to do something like that?*
Hennah:	*Because I'm tired of this farm. Every day is the same. I lay an egg for your breakfast, I help that lazy rooster wake up everyone, and then I wait for you to throw some corn down for me to eat. The highlight of my day is watching Snout the pig roll in the mud! What kind of life is that?*
Farmer C:	*But Hennah, we all love you here. And we'd really miss you if you left. You're an important part of our farm family.*
Hennah:	*But Farmer C, I've just got to see what's out there, away from this farm. I want to meet new animals and see new farms. I want to go to some fun hoedowns and strut until my feet are sore.*
Farmer C:	*Hennah, don't you like your friends here?*
Hennah:	*Yeah, they're nice critters, and Snout doesn't even mind me laughing at him when he's covered in mud.*
Farmer C:	*Well, have I ever let you go hungry?*

Hennah:	*No, not even that time when you had the flu. You sent someone else to feed us.*
Farmer C:	*Haven't I always provided a nice chicken coop for you to nest in?*
Hennah:	*Sure you have. But you don't understand what I'm saying. I'm bored here. I really want to go somewhere else.*
Farmer C:	(Deep sigh) *I sure don't want you to be unhappy here.*
Hennah:	*So, it's okay with you?*
Farmer C:	*I guess so.*
Hennah:	*One last thing, Farmer C.*
Farmer C:	*What's that?*
Hennah:	*Could I have an extra bag of food to take with me for the trip?*

Farmer C: (Disappointedly) *Sure, I'll fix you something right now.* (Puts some corn in a little baggie and hands it to the puppet.)

Hennah: (Grabs the bag and quickly heads off, excitedly talking to herself.) *I'm going to see the world, the beautiful, beautiful world. It's going to be so exciting. Oh, what a beautiful world.*

Farmer C: (Turns to the audience and sadly says) *I'm sorry, kids. You didn't really get to meet Hennah. She's a wonderful chicken when you get to know her. I don't understand what has gotten into her, wanting to leave and all. I raised her since she came out of an egg. I let her stay in the big house when she was little, and I was even there when she laid her very first egg. Gosh, I am going to miss that little ball of feathers.* (Farmer C hangs his head.)

(Throw feathers up in the air as loud clucks and squawks are heard coming from Hennah.)

Hennah: (Frantically appears) Farmer C, Farmer C, Farmer C.

Farmer C: *Hennah, you're back! What's the matter?*

Hennah: *Did you know there are great big trucks out on that road? And there are dogs running loose that like to chase chickens? I was right in the middle of teaching an opossum how to cross the road when this truck goes whizzing past. It almost got both of us!*

Farmer C: *Yes, I know all about those things.*

Hennah: *Well, I didn't! It's scary out there. I think I like it much better here, Farmer C.* (crying) *Can I come back? Will you forgive me for wanting to leave?*

Farmer C: *Oh, Hennah, I'm thrilled you came back. This farm isn't the same without you. How would you like to have a hoedown right here tonight to celebrate you coming back?*

Hennah: *And all the animals could come?*

Farmer C: *Sure thing.*

Hennah: *Sounds exciting to me. You're the best farmer ever. Thank you for taking care of me and loving me even when I do things that disappoint you.*

Farmer C: *You're forgiven, Hennah. Now, I'd better start planning this hoedown.*

Hennah: *And I think it's about time for Snout to take a dive in the mud. I sure don't want to miss that action. See you tonight, and I'll come ready to strut until the music stops.*

For more scripts, visit www.warnerpress.org/321.html

DIRECTOR'S NOTES:

Recording your own stories opens up so many new ways stories can be used. I will leave the actual method of technology to you since you know what kind of equipment you have at your disposal. Make sure you consider, though, that you not only have to record it, but the person listening has to have the equipment to be able to play the story. In other words, if you're recording on an outdated audiocassette, don't assume the recipient will have a working audiocassette player for listening. Audio recording has one set of possibilities, while video recording has more options. So, let's look at the variety that recording can offer to storytelling.

AUDIO SET – 1:

Audio recording allows the listener to tap into his or her imagination. Because the visual has been eliminated, the listeners must draw their own mental action pictures from what they are hearing. This makes audio recordings fun to make, because you want to add as many sound effects as possible to create interest. Also, the emotion in the character's voice needs to be over-exaggerated for the story to be communicated adequately.

PROPS:

Here are some ideas for creating fun sound effects:

- Tap large Styrofoam™ cups on a hard surface to make the clip-clop of donkey hooves.

- A group snapping their fingers will sound like rain coming down.

- Rubbing your palms together sounds like the wind whistling through the trees.

- Make the sound of a torrential rain by using a rain stick. If you don't have one, twist a piece of paper (about 20" long) and then coil it inside a paper towel roller. Cover one end of the tube with paper and seal it. Place ½ cup of beans in the tube and then seal the other end.

- If someone sets something down in the story, then set a hard object down on the table.

- When someone comes in the door, find a noisy door and record its creak.

- A crash can be depicted by using a large tin popcorn container, like you get at Christmas. Fill it with broken dishes, screws, old keys, etc. Then, shake when you want the crash.

- Use one of the plastic baseball bats called a Big Bat to hit against something for a "thud."

- Use a slide whistle to depict someone going up or coming down (like Zacchaeus in the tree).

- For battles, use the long-handled spoons and spatulas from your kitchen and hit the handles against one another.

Acting out as you record is helpful. Everything you touch, pick up, set down, or move probably makes a sound. Exaggerate what you hear or get the microphone close to it, so the sound becomes a key part of the recording. A great way to get the creative juices flowing in kids is to let them listen to an old radio show and list the sound effects they hear. They'll be anxious to create their own once they get started.

DIRECTOR'S NOTES:

There are several ways you can use recordings. As the leader, you can record the story beforehand then allow the kids to listen while you're setting up for or cleaning up from another activity. If you're very self-conscious of acting in front of kids, this may be a great storytelling option you can do in private.

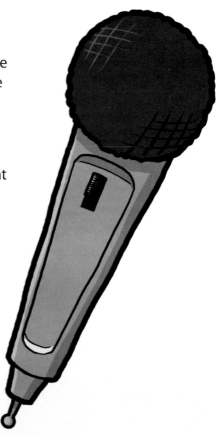

Another option is that the story can be recorded by junior and senior high youth, each one taking on a special role or voice. What a great project and ministry for them! You could even build into your schedule that the youth would provide a pre-recorded story once a quarter. Give them the stories and plenty of time to prepare and get creative. (Don't forget to preview for any excessive liberties they may have taken.)

AUDIO SET – 2:

Another way to do audio recording is to let the kids you are teaching retell the story. Recruit a helper to run the equipment, then find a place outside the classroom to record. Each child can go to the recording area while other activities are taking place, and record his or her special telling of the story. Or, break the story into scenes and assign a child, or several children, to the telling of that scene. One child may do the talking while the others do sound effects. Or, they may want to create the entire scene as dialogue and take on the role of specific characters, much like a play. So many options!

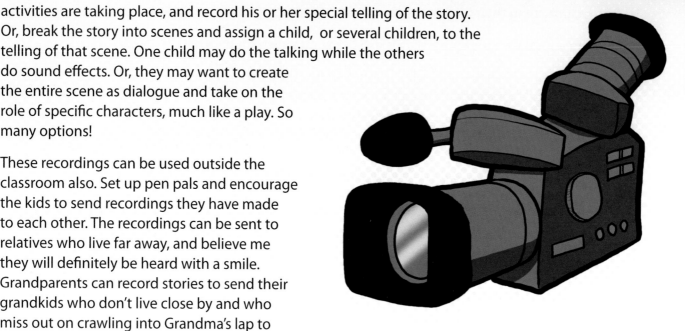

These recordings can be used outside the classroom also. Set up pen pals and encourage the kids to send recordings they have made to each other. The recordings can be sent to relatives who live far away, and believe me they will definitely be heard with a smile. Grandparents can record stories to send their grandkids who don't live close by and who miss out on crawling into Grandma's lap to cuddle and listen.

Video recording leaves less to the imagination of the listener, but more to the imagination of the one being taped. One of the benefits of this kind of recording is that it can be broken down into scenes and taped in short segments. At the end of each scene, actors can change costumes if necessary and sets can be rearranged. It's fun to include creative signs indicating the title of the next scene. Older elementary kids would love spending a couple of weeks putting together an entire videotaped story.

DIRECTOR'S NOTES:

Here's what this storytelling technique could look like in a class of third, fourth, or fifth graders. Instead of the teacher being the one to instruct, the teacher becomes the provider of resources. Before diving into the particulars of recording the story, the children need to become very familiar with every part of it and how one scene affects the other. So, provide them with a variety of Bible storybooks that tell this story. Refer them to an easy-to-read translation of the Bible to read the actual scripture, and maybe even watch a cartoon video of the story to get some ideas.

Then break the kids into groups: some will write, others will be in charge of costumes, sets, signs and acknowledgements. You may be thinking, "This would take all my Sunday school time for two weeks and I wouldn't get to the other activities." You're right and that's okay. This experience will make such an impression on the kids involved that they will never forget the story. They are making it their own, and no craft or puzzle is going to have as much impact. Just like every storytelling technique, overuse is bad use. So, presenting this opportunity to the students once or maybe twice a year will make it very special each time.

There are other opportunities to use what the kids have created. Younger grades would delight to see their older brothers and sisters in a video. Using the video as a special presentation during corporate worship would be a unique way of sharing with the congregation how the children are learning. Send it to a class at another church and encourage them to return a story they put together for you to view. It is important to make sure that the video is shown to someone outside the group of kids who made it.

Reward the class by serving popcorn and pop while they view their masterpiece together.

STORIES THAT WORK WELL WITH VIDEO RECORDING:

- Jesus Feeds the Crowd (Matthew 14:13-23, Mark 6:30-46, Luke 9:10-17, John 6:1-15)

- Esther Saves Her People (Esther 1-10)

- Naaman Is Helped by a Slave Girl (2 Kings 5:1-14)

- David Runs from Saul (1 Samuel 20-28 and 31)

- Ruth (Ruth 1—4)

DIRECTOR'S NOTES:

Sticker Bingo is a very effective way of engaging children in the story as it is being told, with an added bonus that at the end, the kids will get to participate in a game they've created. The game is a form of bingo and will serve as a story reinforcement activity.

PROPS:

- For each story you will need a blank bingo grid, which can be the traditional 5 x 5 squares or it can be a 4 x 4 grid. You'll learn to make your choice by the number of people and things you can identify in the story. I find that the 4 x 4 is usually plenty.

  - To download a 5 x 5, 4 x 4, or 3 x 3 blank grid, go to www.dltk-cards.com/bingo and then click on the "blank" choice at the bottom.

  - Follow the directions. They even have ideas for using the custom cards with groups of fifteen or more. On step 2 you may choose from a long list of theme possibilities, or for this technique, click "Blank" at the bottom. There are several more "steps" that allow you to customize your cards. The program will even print out a "call sheet." DLTK does have a religious Christmas set and some other Bible sets available.

- The Christmas story is available at Christian bookstores in several different sets of stickers, but it's unusual to find other specific Bible story stickers. So, use the computer, a 1" or 1 ½" round label template, and some clip art to create your own story stickers. For the story of Jesus' birth, you would need individual stickers for Joseph, Mary, baby in the manger, stable, angel, many angels, star, shepherd, sheep, 3 individual wise men (wearing different colors or somehow distinguishable), cow, donkey and 2 camels in different positions. Each child will receive a blank bingo grid with the title of the story printed at the top and a set of stickers.

- As the story is told, the children will add stickers to their bingo grid when they hear the person, place, or object mentioned. The storyteller should pause, identify the sticker that should be added, and wait until all have placed their sticker on their grid. It is very important that each child create a unique board, so encourage the children to place their sticker wherever they want, and not to do it like their neighbor.

DIRECTOR'S NOTES:

Making a set of bingo cards is very time consuming because each one has to be different. When the children apply the stickers to create a unique board, they have done all the work for you, but more importantly, in the process have learned so much about the story.

NO CLIP ART? THEN DRAW!

You have two additional options with this technique. Instead of preparing the stickers for the children, let them draw each object on a sticker at the beginning of your session and then place their homemade stickers on the grid as the story is told. Or, you can forego the stickers and the children can draw directly on the grid. There are several drawbacks to using the technique this way, however.

- The children aren't sure how what they're drawing connects to the story if it's done before the story is told.

- You'll find that the children lose the flow of the story because they are spending so much time with crayons or markers, if they draw as the story is told.

NO PICTURES? USE WORDS.

Children who are reading and writing well can write key words on their grid instead of adding stickers or drawing as the items are mentioned in the story. The storyteller should pause at the key word (object), write it on a board where everyone can see and then wait until everyone is finished writing before moving on.

NOW IT'S TIME TO PLAY!

- Give each child enough markers to cover all the squares in the grid, even though they won't need that many. The markers can be pennies, beans, macaroni or small individual candies. For the story of Jesus' birth, we used red and green M&Ms™ and then, as a treat, the kids could eat their markers when the game was over.

- Each sticker, picture or word needs to be on an individual "call" card, to be drawn during the game. Call out what is on the drawn card so the children can cover that item on their board. Before moving on, though, ask one of the children to identify the significance of that item to the story. Great reinforcement!

SKIT 1 - Creation (Genesis 1:1—2:24)

Ideas for stickers: sun, moon, stars, water, circle that is half black and half white, clouds, grass, trees, flowers, fish, birds, 3 different animal stickers, man, woman.

SKIT 2 - Elijah and the Prophets of Baal (1 Kings 18:17-40)

Ideas for stickers: someone dancing, someone shouting, someone asleep, knife, wood, stones, fire, Elijah, bull, shovel, water, jar, king, someone praying, altar, idol, 450, 12.

SKIT 3 - David and Goliath (1 Samuel 17:1-54)

Ideas for stickers: boy, slingshot, 5 stones, 1 stone, lion, bear, bag, giant, sheep, army, king, tent, brook, 2 mountains, armor, sword, spear, shield, bread, cheese, soldiers.

SKIT 4 - Paul Is Shipwrecked (Acts 27:1—28:10)

Ideas for stickers: ship, chains, soldiers, winter, travel chest, angel, waves, ropes, food, broken pieces of ship, 276, campfire, sticks, snake, hand, someone praying.

SKIT 5 - Jesus Rides into Jerusalem (Matthew 21:1-11; Mark 11:1-11; Luke 19:29-40; John 12:12-19)

Ideas for stickers: donkey, colt, rope, 2 disciples, cloaks, palm branches, dirt road, rocks, temple, gate, village, Jesus riding on the colt, someone shouting, crowd, palm trees, children.

DIRECTOR'S NOTES:

Stories appropriate for the story bag technique are those that have a variety of items mentioned. These items are gathered beforehand, placed in a bag (a pillowcase works great), and are used as prompts for telling the story.

PROPS:

- Since many of the actual objects aren't available (like a sheep), something that can act as a clue to it works as a substitute (such as a toy sheep, bookmark with a sheep on it, photo of sheep grazing, or a sheep puppet). The ideas are only limited by the places you're willing to look to scavenge clues.

- The children should gather around the teacher who is holding the bag. The first item is pulled out of the bag and the children identify what it is. From that point, the storyteller relates it to the story. Once that part of the story has been told, before moving on, the next item that will serve as a clue is pulled from the bag. Continue doing this throughout the story.

- The hardest part of this technique is remembering which item comes next, so it's best to make a little cheat sheet to refer to as you go, or you might find yourself with extra pieces when the story is over.

MORE PROPS:

- Don't limit yourself to a pillowcase or grocery bag.

- Baskets, boxes, a tub, even eggs could hold the objects.

- Check out this elephant box. When the storyteller is ready to move to the next object, he or she places the object in the back of the elephant box. One of the children is chosen to reach into the box through the elephant's nose to pull out the next object.

The elephant box is made by covering a medium-size box with grey felt. Leave the back open. Cut a hole where the nose goes about 5" in diameter. The nose is one sleeve of a grey sweatshirt.

DIRECTOR'S NOTES:

I'm going to share a couple of stories that I use with the story bag technique. The items that are mentioned are ones I have in my resources. You may not have these exact items. In that case, you can do one of two things: substitute another idea, using what you do have available, or skip over that object.

SKIT 1 - Joseph in Prison (Genesis 39:19—40:23)

PROPS:

Put these in the story bag: giant key ring with key, silver platter, baker's hat, bunch of grapes, a fancy goblet, 3 baskets, dinner rolls, stuffed bird, party hat and a piece of string.

SCENE 1:

Pull the first item out of the story bag. (I have a large metal ring with a giant key on it that looks like it came from a jail in the Old West.)

- *This key reminds me of a key used for a jail cell. The main person in our story today was a man named Joseph and he had been thrown into prison for something he didn't do. Joseph could've spent his days and nights being angry about having to be in prison and pouting the whole time, but that's not what he did. Instead, Joseph decided to be cheerful and helpful. He did everything he could to make the prison a better place for everyone and soon Joseph was put in complete charge of the prisoners.*

SCENE 2:

Pull out a silver platter and a baker's hat.

- *During this time, the Pharaoh became angry with his butler* (hold up the platter) *and his baker* (put on the hat). *He had both of them thrown into the prison where Joseph was in charge. As with all the prisoners, Joseph got to know these men. One morning Joseph noticed that something seemed to be troubling both of them. When he asked what was wrong, the men said they each had a strange dream that night and didn't know what the dreams meant. God had helped Joseph understand dreams before, so the men shared their dreams.*

This is what the butler said:

SCENE 4:

Pull out a bunch of grapes.

- *In my dream there was a grapevine with three branches. On the branches were clusters of beautiful grapes.* (Pull out a fancy goblet.) *I took the grapes and squeezed them to make juice to serve the Pharaoh.*

- *Joseph said the three branches stood for three days and that in three days the butler would be back at the palace serving the Pharaoh. This made the butler very happy. Joseph pleaded with the butler to remember to give a message to the Pharaoh from him. The message told Pharaoh that Joseph had been sold as a slave and then put in prison for something he didn't do. The butler promised to deliver the message. When the baker heard the good news Joseph gave the butler, he was anxious to tell Joseph his dream.* (Pull out 3 baskets with bread in one of them.) *The baker told Joseph that in his dream there were three baskets on his head and there was bread in the top basket.*

Pull out a stuffed bird.

- *The birds flew down and ate the bread out of the top basket. God helped Joseph understand this dream also, but the news wasn't so good for the baker. Joseph didn't want to tell the baker what it meant, because in three days the Pharaoh would have the baker killed.*

SCENE 4:

Pull out a party hat.

- *Three days later there was a huge birthday party for the Pharaoh. During the party, the Pharaoh called for his butler to return to his job. He also told his soldiers to hang the baker.*

SCENE 5:

Pull out a piece of string and tie it around your finger.

> • *A long time ago people used to wear a piece of string around their finger to remind them to do something they were afraid they would forget. Joseph should've tied a string around the butler's finger, because he forgot all about his promise to tell the Pharaoh about Joseph being in prison for no reason. It was two years before the butler remembered to mention Joseph to the Pharaoh.*

SKIT 2 - The Birth of Jesus (Luke 2:1-39, along with Matthew 2)

DIRECTOR'S NOTES:

• Kids love to open presents, so turn some wrapped gifts into containers for story bag objects. Because the gifts need to be opened in order, after they're wrapped, write a number on them to indicate their position in the sequence. Place the gifts under a Christmas tree and call on one child at a time to find the gift with the next number on it. Let each child enjoy unwrapping the gift and identifying what he or she discovered inside.

PROPS:

#1 box **Watch**
"At that time," was a special
time in history when a census was
being taken throughout the entire Roman world. Explain census.

#2 box **Piece of bread**
Bread reminds us that Bethlehem means "house of bread." Joseph and Mary traveled to the "house of bread," Bethlehem, because everyone was told to enroll in the town where their family came from. Joseph's family was from Bethlehem.

#3 box **Baby doll**
When they arrived in Bethlehem, it was time for Mary to have her baby. Because the city was crowded, there was no place for them to stay. The only place they could find was a stable, and that's where Baby Jesus was born.

#4 box   **Soft cloth**
When the baby was born, Mary wrapped Him in soft cloths.

#5 box   **Cotton balls, sheep sticker, sheep puppet, or a sheep photo**
Out on the hillsides around Bethlehem there were shepherds watching their sheep.

#6 box   **Halo made out of gold chenille stick or some gold tinsel**
An angel surprised the shepherds and startled them. The angel told them that they shouldn't be afraid and that they should go find a special baby who had just been born in Bethlehem. The baby was the Savior they had been waiting for, and they would find Him wrapped in cloths and lying in a manger.

#7 box   **Newspaper heading with great news**
This was wonderful news for the shepherds!

#8 box   **Hay**
The shepherds left their sheep and went to find the baby. They found Him in a manger filled with hay, in a stable, just as the angels had told them.

#9 box   **Cutout heart or a heart-shaped ornament**
Mary remembered everything that happened and kept each memory in her heart.

#10 box   **Star**
In a faraway country there were wise men who studied the stars and noticed a new star in the sky.

#11 box   **Map**
The wise men followed the star and traveled to Bethlehem where it was leading them.

#12 box   **Scroll**
The wise men remembered that the prophets had written that a Savior would be born in Bethlehem.

#13 box   **Gift**
The wise men gave Baby Jesus gifts of gold, frankincense and myrrh.

OTHERS STORIES TO USE WITH STORY BAG TECHNIQUE:

- Paul Is Shipwrecked (Acts 27—28:10) – Items: handcuffs, model ship, anchors, scissors, broken up craft sticks, match, snake, Band-aids™.

- A Wife for Isaac (Genesis 23:1—25:18) – Items: camel(s), pitcher, 2 gold bracelets, food to eat (cheese and bread), clothing, veil.

- Josiah Finds God's Book (2 Chronicles 34:1—35:19) – Items: crown, cleaning rag, piece of wood, a stone, scroll, picture of an ear or a plastic ear (never heard), piece of ripped clothing, bitter herbs and/or unleavened bread (Passover).

See more Story Bag ideas online at www.warnerpress.org/321.html

DIRECTOR'S NOTES:

Dig it out of a cobweb-filled closet—you know what I'm talking about—the overhead projector. PowerPoint® was so easily mastered that overhead projectors were abandoned overnight. I'm a master, though, at resurrecting things that have been discarded and making them into something useful for children's ministry. And so, let me show you how the overhead projector can once again be useful— in storytelling.

PROPS:

Bible costumes are great and help kids identify with the character, but actually putting together a setting or environment to go along with the costumed character takes a lot more time and work. When done well, settings are a marvelous thing and the overhead projector can provide you a shortcut. Transparencies can be made of different settings and, when projected on a large blank wall, will create the environment you're looking for. We've provided a few ideas here, but you can create more of your own. For those of you who are not artistically inclined, I'll include some tips on how you too can make additional scenes.

- Copy background scenes from the ideas at the end of this section onto transparency sheets. Make sure the packaging states the sheets can be run through your model of copier. Otherwise, although it takes a little more time, go back to the old-fashioned way and trace them.

- Once the outline is done, you can use it as is or take it one step further and color parts of the scene.

- Always use permanent markers or specially made markers for overhead projectors (Vis-à-vis markers). Because markers take a few moments to dry on the plastic sheets, start in the upper left corner of the scene (if you're right-handed) and work your way down and across. That will keep your hand from dragging through the fresh ink and smearing it.

- When you're drawing your background scenery, keep it fairly simple and make it the size of the full transparency sheet.

- Bible story coloring books are a great place to find additional backgrounds for those of you who don't think highly of your artistic talents. When tracing the pictures, leave out the people and connect the lines that are missing.

- Bible story clip art books are another great source for background scenery.

DIRECTOR'S NOTES:

Once the transparency has been made, project the scenery onto a large blank wall, preferably white, so the colors of the scene will show up well. You want the scenery to be life-size, so reposition your projector until the scene fits the space correctly. If at all possible, the storyteller then stands at the edge of the projected scene. Getting in the middle of the scene to tell the story is risky, since the projected lines will then be projected onto the storyteller. Oops! That could be funny!

STORING TRANSPARENCIES

- File the transparencies away properly to use at another time.

- Store transparencies with a piece of plain white paper against both sides; the top piece keeps the ink from transferring onto anything in front of it, and the bottom piece helps you see exactly what is on the transparency.

- Next time you need that particular transparency, you'll be so proud of yourself for your efficiency.

SCENERY IDEAS:

- **Palace -** Esther Approaches the King (Esther 5)
  The Queen of Sheba Visits Solomon (1 Kings 10:1-13)

- **Grassy hills (with a stream) -** The Lost Sheep (Matthew 18:12-14, Luke 15:3-7)
  Jonathan Warns David (1 Samuel 20)

- **The inside of a house -** A Room for Elisha (2 Kings 4:8-17)
  The Coming of the Holy Spirit (Acts 2:1-47)

OTHER SCENES YOU CAN INCLUDE IN TRANSPARENCIES:

- Cave
- Prison
- Ship
- Seaside
- Tent

ALTERNATIVE: TRANSPARENCY STORIES

An additional way to use that overhead projector, other than for a doorstop, is to use it totally for the storytelling. Instead of reading from a book, copy the pages of a Bible story coloring book. Warner Press has delightful ones that are reproducible.

- Give each child one of the pictures to color. Instructions for copying them on transparencies are the same as we gave for coloring background scenery.

- Or, pass out written descriptions of scenes in the story and the children will draw that scene on the transparency.

- As the story is told, the children will display their scene on the overhead projector. What a great way to make a coloring activity meaningful, and the kids absolutely love to show off their work this way. This would also make a great activity for an Open House when parents get to see what the kids have been doing in their class. Each child could tell the part of the story their transparency portrays.

UNIQUE POINT OF VIEW

DIRECTOR'S NOTES:

This is a technique that is fun to play with. Imagine an inanimate or nonhuman object in the story suddenly having a voice and being able to tell what they experienced. Don't get crazy on me. We are not going to change the truth of the story, but merely look at it from a unique point of view. Just as we might imagine how we would've felt or what we would've done if we'd been there, we can imagine what a rock, or a donkey, or a piece of red cord may have seen, heard and even felt as they witnessed these phenomenal stories of God's faithfulness.

PROPS:

It's not necessary to wear anything special or create an environment, but don't discard that idea completely. There always seems to be one more thing to add that would spice up the story. For instance:

Artistic License

Stories told well paint a mental picture for the listener. Your voice, props and sound effects are the paintbrush that makes the picture come alive. Have you ever watched a television program where someone walks you through painting a picture? About three-fourths of the way through the teaching, what is being taught starts popping out, making sense and coming to life. When you merely read a story, it's like painting that picture about three-fourths of the way, then stopping. Inflection, props, sound effects and all the other things added to the story make it really come to life.

- As the rock in the story of David and Goliath, put down a blue plastic tablecloth for the stream and maybe a couple of large rocks along the edge. Lie next to the plastic as the story begins, sunning yourself.

- As the red cord in the story of Rahab and the Spies, wear all red that day.

DIRECTOR'S NOTES:

Then, let your body also convey what's happening.

- When the small stone is put down in David's pouch, get into a tight fetal position and peek out through your fingers. When the stone is flung through the air, hold your hands out, fingers spread wide apart, and have a terrified look on your face, as if you're about to experience the biggest roller coaster you've ever been on.

- If you're dangling from the window as the red cord, then put your hands over your head and swiggle (that's swaying and wiggling together).

- In short, avoid just reading the story, because it loses its umph! Instead, be the rock...be the red cord...be the fleece...be Balaam's donkey.

Here are some questions you can ask yourself as you prepare to tell a story from a Unique Point of View.

- What relationship does the object have with the main character?

- Where is the object usually kept? Where is its home? What does it look like, feel like?

- What emotions could the object have had concerning what it was called upon to do?

- How can you portray the movement of the object?

- What happens to the object when the story comes to an end?

- How will you imitate the sound the object makes on its own when it moves, or when it touches something else?

- Is the object looking up at or down at the action? What is the vantage point?

- Does the object relate to other similar objects and how is that done?

SCRIPT 1 - The Red Cord (Rahab Helps the Spies – Joshua 1—2 and 5:13—6:27)

DIRECTOR'S NOTES:

The object telling the story is the red cord, which was instrumental in identifying Rahab's house when the Israelites invaded Jericho. Even though the cord is not actually used until the end of the story, it observes what is happening and the conversations that take place throughout.

SCENE 1:

- *Rahab, the lady who owned the house, was working on a new piece of cloth. The loom was set up and there were many beautiful colors of cording that would become part of it. I knew, because I was one of them. In the large basket that sat next to the loom was the assortment of cords. It wouldn't be long now before I took my place in the loom, because I was now lying at the top of the basket. To be part of something so beautiful as the piece of cloth Rahab was making was an honor. I couldn't wait to see how I fit in with the others.*

SCENE 2:

- *Two strangers came to our house one day. They had just entered the city through the main gate, and Rahab's house was actually part of the wall to the city. The two men were Israelites—the enemy—but Rahab talked with them anyway. Somehow, Rahab knew that the Lord was with these men. While they were talking, there was a knock at the door. It was the king's soldiers and they were looking for the Israelite spies.*

- *I've never seen Rahab in such a hurry; I saw her hustle the men up to the roof. That's where she hid them, in a big pile of flax. When she let the soldiers in, they searched everywhere. They even went through the basket of cords that I was in. The Lord really was with the men, just like Rahab thought, because the soldiers never thought to look through the flax on the roof.*

- *Rahab told the soldiers that she had seen the men, but when she saw them they were going out the gate. I heard her tell them to hurry after the Israelite strangers and the soldiers did.*

SCENE 3:

- *When the Israelite men came down off the roof, they talked with Rahab about their God. Rahab recognized that God was with the Israelites.*

- *Before the men left to go back to their camp, Rahab asked them for a favor. She knew that the Israelites were going to take over the city of Jericho, but she asked if there was a way that her family could be spared. The men looked at each other and then promised to help her. One of the men reached over to the basket where I was and grabbed hold of me. Whoa-oa-oa-oa! He was dangling me high in the air. I don't think I like this! It's kind of scary out here. Then the Israelite man said, "Hang this red cord from your window and the Israelite soldiers will know where you and your family are. We will send someone for you."*

SCENE 4:

- As soon as they left, Rahab hung me out the window. Since Rahab's house was part of the wall of the city of Jericho, I could see forever as I hung there. But, would I lose my place in becoming part of the fabric on the loom? Somehow, that didn't matter. My job of hanging out the window seemed pretty important to Rahab.

SCENE 5:

- A few days later strange things started happening outside the wall of Jericho. The Israelites marched up to the wall but they didn't do anything. I was all ready for the fighting to break out. The tension was thick in the air. Well, I said they didn't do anything…that isn't exactly true…it just seemed like nothing.

- They were marching around the city. There were a whole bunch of soldiers in the front. And then there were priests playing rams' horns. At the very end were some men carrying a box on poles with all the rest of the Israelite people walking behind it. They marched around the city and then went back to camp.

SCENE 6:

- All night I thought about what I had seen. It was so strange. What could it mean?

- The sun came up the next day and guess what? The Israelites came back, and they did the same thing all over again, just like the day before.

- I just hung there outside Rahab's window watching. They walked around the city, blew their horns, carried the box, and then went home. I counted and they did that for six days. Every day the same thing!

SCENE 7:

- There was a lot going on outside, but there was also lots going on inside Rahab's house. She must have realized the Israelites were about to attack, because she went to get her father and mother and all her brothers and sisters. They would act like they were going to go home, but Rahab wouldn't let them leave. They all watched out the window where I hung and saw everything that was happening.

SCENE 8:

- On the seventh day it started even earlier. I saw the Israelites go around the city once and I thought they would head back to camp. But it was different that day. They kept marching around the city.

- One…two…three…four…five…six…seven!

- When they finished going around the city seven times, they started blowing their horns. My goodness, it was loud! And then all the Israelites started shouting at the top of their lungs. I had never heard such a noise!

- Things started shaking. The ground seemed to be moving. I saw stones that were part of the wall start falling to the ground. Everything around me was turning to rubble. How could this be? The Israelites didn't touch anything; they just played their horns and shouted. God was helping the Israelites and I got to watch it all happen. What a day!

SCENE 9:

- The thought did cross my mind—what's going to happen to me now? I'm hanging here and our city is being destroyed. I'll be forgotten in the rubble. What's going to happen to Rahab?

- Just about that time, the two Israelite spies who Rahab had hidden from the king's soldiers came into the house. I heard them say, "We saw the red cord in the window and knew where to find you. Come quickly, we'll take you to safety." They had come for Rahab and her family just like they promised they would. The family grabbed a few bags and headed out the door with the Israelite men.

SCENE 10:

- I hung there. The house was quiet now. I was happy that Rahab and her family were safe, but I was still hanging in the window…feeling a little sorry for myself.

- Then, I saw Rahab come back in the house. She hurried to the window where I was hanging and pulled me in. Down in her bag I went, and as she put me there I heard her say quietly to herself, "This little red cord will hang in my new home to remind me of how God worked in a mighty way this day."

SCRIPT 2 - The Rod (God Chooses Aaron – Numbers 17)

SCENE 1:

- I considered myself just one of many rods; we were all pretty much the same. Some people might think that we're just big sticks, but there's more to us than that.

- When my buddies and I passed each other as we went from one duty to another, we'd yell a rod greeting. "Hey, where you headed? Saved my master last night! Pretty day for a walk." We never knew what we might be called upon to do.

SCENE 2:

- Right off the top of my rod (or head) I can think of several things we're used for. Anytime the men gather around to talk, you'll find many of them leaning on their rod. We're handy and strong and always seem to be there when someone needs to be held up.

- A friend of mine is a special kind of rod and he's helped rescue sheep that have fallen in a hole or gotten caught in thorny bushes. I guess you could say that he's a rescuing rod.

- I had the chance one time to be a weapon when a lion came into the camp. Several of us clubbed that lion until he ran away to find a meal somewhere else.

- *Then, there are everyday things that we get used for. When something needs to be measured, it's easy to lay down the rod and figure out about how long it is or how much material is needed.*
- *I've never done this, but I've heard that some rods get used on the threshing floor to separate the grain from the chaff. Listening to all of this, I just wonder how men could ever get along without us!*

SCENE 3:

- *There's one other thing that special rods get to do and that is stand beside important men. A handsome staff is the sign of someone who has authority and should be respected.*
- *Such was the case one day when Moses gathered twelve of us together. He very carefully carved the name of the leader of each of the twelve tribes into a rod. As he carved, Moses talked about how God had told him to do this, but he wasn't sure how it was going to help.*
- *You see, God had put Moses in charge of the Israelite people and they were sometimes difficult to lead. They complained a lot, to say the very least.*
- *In me, Moses carved the name of Aaron, his brother, because Aaron was the head of the tribe of Levi.*

SCENE 4:

- *After Moses had the names carved into all twelve rods, he carefully picked us up and carried us into the tabernacle. I'd never been in there and it was an absolutely beautiful place. This was where the Israelites went to worship and I could see why they thought it was so special. The tabernacle was the place they had built for God. Then, we went behind a curtain into another part of the tabernacle. It was quiet and the light was low there. There was a beautiful golden box that Moses called the ark sitting in the middle of this special place.*
- *Moses gently laid all twelve of us on the ground in front of this magnificent box, and then…he left. Was this our new home? Were we done doing the other things that rods do? Was it just going to be the twelve of us rods and the golden box forever?*

SCENE 5:

- *Something strange started happening to me in the middle of the night. I felt kind of tingly, like something was moving inside me. What was happening? I whispered in the dark to the other rods and called them by the names that had been carved in them. "Do you feel anything?" I questioned them. Each time the answer came back that nothing was happening and I should just relax for the night.*

SCENE 6:

- *In the morning, though, when the light was brighter, it was pretty clear that something had happened to me in the night. Blossoms had grown from me, and it looked like I had become part of a tree again. The blossoms were beautiful! I was beautiful! Wow, this was so cool.*

- *"Hey guys, look at this!" I said to the others. They definitely weren't as excited as I was. As I looked around, nothing had happened to anyone else. Now I was really confused. What was going on here?*

SCENE 7:

- *About that time Moses entered. He carefully looked at all the rods and then picked me up. He turned me around so that he could read the name that had been carved into my side. It read, "Aaron." Moses seemed very happy about that and I could hear him say, "Just as God said."*

- *Then, Moses picked us all up and carried us out of the tabernacle. I guess our stay there was over. "Good-bye, beautiful place."*

SCENE 8:

- *The Israelites gathered and Moses put all twelve of us on display for them to see.*

- *The people kept asking what had happened to me. Then, I found out what this was all about. God had told Moses to do this—to carve the names of the leaders of the tribes in the rods.*

- *God had told Moses to put all twelve of us in the tabernacle in front of the ark, and that one of the rods would bloom. That's me!*

- *God told Moses that the rod that bloomed would be the rod of the man He had chosen to be the high priest. That's Aaron! It was a sign from God. I was a part of a sign from God! How amazing is that!*

SCENE 9:

- *The other rods were given back to the leaders of the other tribes, but I didn't go back to Aaron. There was one more thing that God wanted to do with me.*

- *God told Aaron to place me back in the tabernacle where the people would be reminded that He had chosen Aaron as His priest. If there were ever any question, the people would see me standing there and remember how God had chosen Aaron.*

OTHER STORIES THAT CAN BE TOLD FROM A UNIQUE POINT OF VIEW:

- Fleece - Gideon and the Fleece (Judges 6:33-40)

- Rock in the stream - David and Goliath (1 Samuel 17:1-54)

- Two coins - A Widow Gives All (Mark 12:41-44)

- Donkey - Balaam's Donkey Speaks (Numbers 22:1-35)

- Bottle of oil - A Woman Anoints Jesus' Feet (Luke 7:36-50)

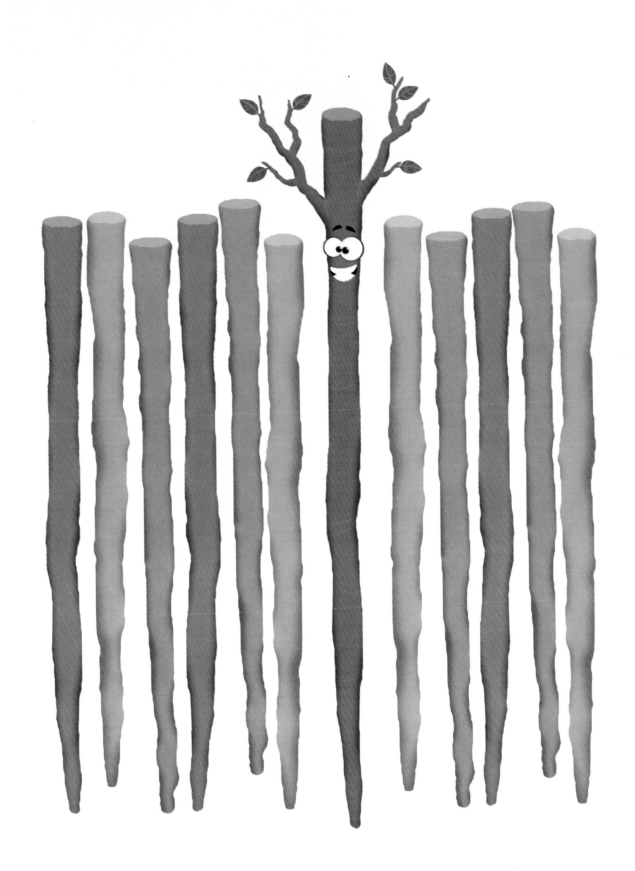

DIRECTOR'S NOTES:

Videos are a nice alternative technique in storytelling, but they come with a bright yellow caution tag.

- Videos are so easy and convenient that they can trap the person who is prone to last minute preparation. Hence, when Saturday evening comes and the teacher finds himself tired from a day's activities and staring at a blank page, it's a relief to go to the video cabinet and pull out something, whether or not it fits into the scope and sequence of what that lesson is trying to teach.

- Videos need to be used with the same intentionality and forethought as any other technique. Keep that in mind and videos can be excellent tools.

- An extra benefit to using videos—they can be tremendously helpful when a less experienced person is filling in for an absent teacher.

PREVIEW THIS PROP:

Always preview the video in its entirety before showing it to the children. There are several reasons for this:

- First of all, you need to make sure the video covers the part of the story you want to teach. You may find you only want to watch a portion of it then finish watching it a week or two later when the rest of the story comes up in your curriculum scope and sequence.

- Also, you'll want to time the video to make sure it fits in the time you have allotted with the kids. The ending of the video is when everything comes together, so you don't want parents pulling kids out before they have seen it all.

- Previewing also gives you an opportunity to mark any places where you might want to break for discussion.

- Lastly, while previewing you can write up specific questions for other activities that may follow.

USING THE PROP:

- If you have the capabilities, project the video onto a plain white wall to make it as large as possible.

- Move the kids out of their chairs and onto the floor.

- Provide plenty of pillows to create a cozy atmosphere. If you know far enough in advance that you'll be showing a video, publicize it by telling the kids they'll need to bring their own pillows and house slippers for class, but don't let on that it's a video. Kids are usually glued to a video, but one way to increase their concentration is by giving each child a set of cards about the video.

- To make cards:

  - When you preview the video, make note of some small details you notice in the story. It might be a bird soaring overhead, a mouse scurrying through the barn, a broom sitting in the corner of a room, or a sleeping baby. Each card will have one of these written on it.

  - Before the video is shown, the kids will organize their cards in whatever manner makes sense to them.

  - They'll then be watching for those specific items found on their cards. When spot one, have them remove that card and put it in their found pile.

RECOMMENDED VIDEOS

The K-10-C Video series teaches The Ten Commandments (Exodus 19—24) and is available at www.k10c.com. These cartoons are such high quality my kids frequently find them being shown on television.

The Greatest Adventure Bible Story series by Hanna-Barbera covers a wide variety of stories, both Old and New Testament.

Nest Entertainment offers different set sizes of Bible stories; DVDs can be purchased in a set of 12, 24, 36, 56 or 74 stories. Told in cartoon format the videos can be purchased in sets, individually or with study resources from www.nestentertainment.com.

This Is a Test!
Test your props and equipment. Run through the story to make sure that props are where you placed them, that the microphone or any equipment you are relying on is available and working properly and that the platform/audience seating is organized for best possible results. If you're going to rely on prompts or notes for any part of the story, are they out of view of the audience, but easy for you to see?

DIRECTOR'S NOTES:

This word response technique can work in a couple of ways. Involving kids in the story telling in an active way increases their ability to focus and strengthens their learning skills.

TECHNIQUE 1:

- The audience is given a word or phrase that they are to say each time they are cued.

- At certain points in the story, the storyteller will indicate that the audience should respond with their word or phrase.

- Reaction words such as *yummy, yippee, cool, yuck, yikes, whoa, woo-hoo, shhhh* and *bummer* can be written on cards with instructions for the kids to say the response word each time the card is lifted.

TECHNIQUE 2:

- Another way to use word response is to indicate words the group will listen for as the story is told.

- When they hear these trigger words, they respond with a motion or a sound (or both).

- The entire group can listen for all the words or you can break the class into smaller groups so each of them is listening for one particular word to respond to.

SKIT 1 - Birth of Jesus (Luke 2:1-39)

- Trigger Words: *sheep, angels* and *baby.*

- Divide the children into three groups.

- The first group will listen for the word "sheep." Each time they hear sheep mentioned in the story, they will immediately start saying "baa-baa."

- The second group will respond to the word "angels" by holding their arms out like wings and saying "Fear not!" (We all know that's what angels say).

- The last group listens for the word "baby" and sucks their thumb while crying "whaaa-whaaa" each time they hear it.

Turn It Up!

Turn up your enthusiasm. Turn up your passion. Turn up your conviction to communicate the truth of God's Word. If you're excited about telling the story, you've increased the possibility that the kids will be excited about listening to it.

SKIT 2 - Jacob and Rachel (Genesis 19:1-28)

- Prepare two signs: one that reads *"Oh, yes!"* and the other *"Oh, no!"*

- Choose two children to hold the signs in front of the group.

- Instruct the kids to respond by saying what is written on the sign being held high.

- When you come to a place in the story where a sign should be raised, tap the shoulder of the appropriate child.

SCENE 1:

Teacher: *Jacob had traveled a long way and he must have been tired.*

Kids: *Oh, yes!*

Teacher: *Off in the distance he could see a well. Surrounding the well were lots of sheep and their shepherds. Jacob thought he must be getting close to his uncle's home. When he got closer to the well, he asked the shepherds waiting there if they knew a man named Laban.*

Kids: *Oh, yes!*

Teacher: *Not only did they know him, but they pointed to a young woman named Rachel who was coming close to them with her sheep. They said she was Laban's daughter. Jacob was so glad to see her.*

Kids: *Oh, yes!*

Teacher: *He hoped his journey was over. He lifted the stone that covered the well and watered the sheep for her. When he had finished he told Rachel who he was. Rachel was so excited she ran off to find her father and tell him that she had met Jacob and he was at the well.*

Kids: *Oh, yes!*

Teacher: *Laban dropped everything he was doing and went to the well to meet his nephew.*

SCENE 2:

Teacher: Jacob stayed with Laban and took care of his sheep. One day Laban approached Jacob about paying him for the work he was doing with the sheep. Jacob said instead of being paid, he would work for Laban for seven years if he could marry Rachel.

Kids: Oh, yes!

Teacher: Jacob worked hard for Laban, and the seven years seemed to pass quickly. The wedding plans were made and it was time for Jacob and Rachel to be married. Laban had a problem though.

Kids: Oh, no!

Teacher: Rachel had an older sister, Leah, who was not married yet. It was the custom that the oldest daughter got married first. Laban came up with a plan.

Kids: Oh, no!

Teacher: He had Leah dress in the wedding clothes and the veil. She would marry Jacob without his knowing it.

Kids: Oh, no!

SCENE 3:

Teacher: After the wedding Jacob realized he had married the wrong woman.

Kids: Oh, no!

Teacher: This was not the woman he loved; this was not Rachel!

Kids: Oh, no!

Teacher: Jacob was very angry and went to Laban with his complaint.

SCENE 4:

Teacher: *Laban explained why he had tricked Jacob. He told Jacob that if he worked for another seven years he could marry Rachel also.*

Kids: *Oh, no!*

Teacher: *At that time the law permitted a man to marry more than one woman.*

SCENE 5:

Teacher: *Jacob agreed with Laban's plan, so Jacob married Rachel as well. Now the woman Jacob loved dearly was his wife.*

Kids: *Oh, yes!*

SKIT 3 - Jesus Is Rejected By a Rich Young Man (Matthew 19:16-30)

DIRECTOR'S NOTES:

- Divide the kids into two groups.
- The first group will say *"And Jesus said"* when you point to them.
- The second group will say *"And the man said"* when you point to them.

SCENE 1:

Point to group #1: *And the man said*

Teacher: *How can I have eternal life?*

Point to group #2: *And Jesus said*

Teacher: *Have you kept the commandments?*

Point to group #1: *And the man said*

Teacher: *Which ones?*

Point to group #2: *And Jesus said*

Teacher: *Do not murder. Do not commit adultery. Do not steal. Do not lie. Honor your father and mother. Love your neighbor as yourself.*

Point to group #1: *And the man said*

Teacher: *I do all those things. Is there anything else?*

Point to group #2:	*And Jesus said*
Teacher:	*Then go and sell everything you own and come follow me. If you do this, you'll have treasure in heaven.*
Point to group #1:	*And the man said*
Teacher:	*NOTHING! He didn't say anything! Give away everything he owned? What was Jesus talking about? The man had many beautiful things. People liked to be around him because of the things he owned. The man turned around and sadly walked away from Jesus.*

SCENE 2:

Teacher:	*Jesus talked to His disciples about what had happened with the rich young man. He explained to the disciples that it was very difficult for a rich man to get into heaven because the rich get wrapped up in what they own. He even said it would be easier to get a camel to go through the eye of a needle than it is for a rich man to give up his riches in order to have heaven.*
	Jesus told the disciples that those who give up everything for the kingdom of God will have much in heaven, even though they have very little on earth. The people who seem most important on earth will be least important in heaven. And the people who are least important on earth will be the greatest in heaven.

INDEX

OLD TESTAMENT

NEW TESTAMENT